Developin

As a Bridge to Christianity in Japan

Developing a Contextualized Church As a Bridge to Christianity in Japan

Mitsuo Fukuda

Contents

List of Figures

List of Tables

Preface

Twenty years ago, I wrote this doctoral thesis and returned to Japan to experiment with Japanese Christian rituals, using salt, water, incense and so on.

But now, these forms of worship are naturally emerging within the house church movement. For example, an 81 year old grandmother expresses her worship to Jesus with a song that she wrote herself. Before she became a Christian, she used to write songs and sing them; now that her heart is turned to Jesus, she naturally takes those things that she already knew and uses them to worship him.

This real-life example of contextualization has had nothing to do with missiologists or missiological theory; I believe that the role of the missiologist is, when this kind of example arises, to recognise these things as the work of the Holy Spirit.

Part I

Introduction

Chapter 1

Introduction

Even after more than 400 years of missionary effort in Japan, Christians still make up only 0.7 percent of the Japanese population! One of the major reasons for this lack of effectiveness is a lack of contextualization. Japanese Christianity is like a "potted plant" which has been transported without have been transplanted. Japanese people see Christianity as as a Western religion to which they cannot relate. Japan's intellectual, Westernized Christianity is like a small middle-class ghetto that is almost irrelevant to the reality of most people's lives.

Making a study of the socio-cultural context of the target group is a significant step toward communicating the Gospel. However, as Nishiyama (1991) points out, Christian churches fail to take seriously the indigenous religiosity of modern Japanese: "Experiential religion for the Japanese is rooted in folk religion and the new religions. In my view, neither the Christian churches nor theological education have seriously grappled with this problem in Japan." (1991:10-11) Japanese religions, and in particular their supernatural orientation which is rooted deeply in the religiosity of the masses, have been excluded as "pagan", instead of understood as functioning to serve the felt needs of the people.

Our ecclesiology also has been transported from the West. The great values of Western ecclesiology can be realized only if they are understood as part of an ethno-ecclesiology contextualized to the Western context. These values may address problems that the Japanese also face, but they are primarily designed to answer questions emerging from the Western context. An ethno-ecclesiology needs to be constructed which will answer Japanese questions.

Japanese Christians also need to construct contextual models of Church that communicate the Gospel to the hearts of the Japanese. These models should find their own expression of the Christian life, while at the same time joining in faith and truth with other congregations worldwide under Christ's lordship. We are convinced that the key to evangelizing the Japanese lies in multiplying dynamic, culturally relevant churches.

In seeking to improve the effectiveness of Christian missionaries in Japan, it is necessary to construct new church forms which are both Biblically sound and culturally relevant.

The problem to be addressed in this study is to develop a contextual Japanese church model based upon an ethno-ecclesiology designed to answer Japanese questions, constructed in conjunction with the Biblical text as well as contemporary ecclesiology. The major questions to be addressed by this study are as follows:

1. What is the Japanese worldview and culture?

2. What is Pauline ecclesiology?

3. What is contemporary ecclesiology?

4. What would be an appropriate ethno-ecclesiology for Japan?

5. What would be an appropriate contextual church model for Japan?

In examining Japanese cultural behavior, we have dealt only with the Japanese religious system, and in particular focusing on ritual practices. The central theme for our constructing a contextual church model is contextual ritualization, and thus we need to examine the rituals of Japanese religions. The religious subsystem is deeply interrelated with other cultural subsystems, and the contextualized church needs to interact with all these subsystems, as well as with the more general concept of worldview. A more through analysis of Japanese culture should be made at another time.

Biblical ecclesiology can be viewed from several perspectives. In this study, we have given an overview of Pauline ecclesiology alone. In particular, we have not dealt with the relationship between the Pauline epistles and Acts.

While I understand the study of ethno-ecclesiology in non-Western contexts (e.g. Asia, Africa, South America) may provide rich missiological insights, for the purposes of our inquiry we will only review contemporary Western ecclesiology.

Japanese culture is diversified according to locality, generation, social class, races and the like. The context of the contextualized church cannot be fully categorized by a uniform description. Each local expression of contextual church will need to develop their own communication strategies paying attention to their own unique context. However, in this study we simply give a generalized model of communication.

This study is based on the following assumptions:

- God loves the Japanese people and desires to have a personal relationship with them.

- Only through Jesus Christ is salvation available.

- The Bible is a uniquely authoritative standard.

- God views culture primarily as a vehicle to be used by Him and His people for Christian purposes, rather than as an enemy to be combatted or shunned. (Kraft, 1979:115)

- God exists totally outside of culture while humans exist totally within culture. However, God chooses the cultural milieu in which humans are immersed as the arena of His interaction with people.

- God communicates to the Japanese by employing and transforming the Japanese cultural forms (including their religious forms). Christian communicators can reshape the Christian church in answer to Japanese questions which arise from their worldview. This should be done with Japanese methodologies and terminologies.

1.1   Review of Literature

This study consists of three parts. The first part analyzes the Japanese worldview and their religious rituals. The second part discusses an ethno-ecclesiology for Japan. The third part describes the resulting contextualized model of church. Each part is based upon and guided by precedent literature.

1.1.1   Japanese Worldview and Religious Rituals

Charles H. Kraft (1979; 1989) and Paul G. Hiebert (1983a; 1990), contemporary Christian anthropologists, provide a framework for the discussion of worldview. Morris Opler's concept of "cultural theme" (1946) and Michael Kearney's ideas of "logico-structural integration" and "world-view universal" (1984) have aided in constructing the theory of worldview.

The works of Shigeru Nishiyama (1984; 1988a; 1988b; 1991), Ian Reader (1991), Taichi Sakaiya (1991), Minoru Hayashi (1988) and the Japan Ministry of Culture (1972) are foundational to my approach to Japanese supernaturalism and other worldview themes. Munesuke Mita's idea of "original grace" (1965) provides helpful insights to examine the Japanese "good fortune consciousness." Tokutaro Sakurai (1985) analyzes the structure of Japanese religious festival, which has helped to develop a model of the dynamics of religious ritual in a contextual church.

1.1.2   Toward the Ethno-ecclesiology

Herman Ridderbos (1975) in his study of Pauline theology has been particularly helpful in examining Pauline ecclesiology.

Dean S. Gilliland (1983; 1989), Clinton E. Arnold (1992), Paul D. Hanson (1986), Robert John Banks (1988) and Roland Allen (1962a; 1962b) have also contributed to our analysis of the Pauline idea of community. In dealing with contemporary ecclesiology, we primarily employ the work of Karl Barth (1956; 1958; 1961; 1962) as a framework for discussion. Karl Barth, Emil Brunner (1952; 1949), Dietrich Bonhoeffer (1963; 1971), Hendrikus Berkhof (1986) and Jürgen Moltmann (1977) are the main contributors in this discussion. David J. Bosch (1991) and Charles Edward Van Engen (1991) make sharp critiques on the works of these theologians from the missiological perspective.

1.1.3 A Contextual Church Model for Japan

In developing communication strategies, we integrate Viggo B. Søgaard's "spiritual decision process model" (1989; 1991) and Kraft's "encounters thinking" (1991b), with "approaches to communication." (1991a) Edward R. Dayton and David A. Fraser (1990), Paul G. Hiebert (1978; 1983b; 1990), and James F. Engel and H. Wilbert Norton (1975) provide useful communication models. We employ Hiebert's principle of "critical contextualization" (1984) as the method for developing contextualized rituals.

1.2 Methodology

This study is based on my field experience in Japan as well as on documentary data analysis. As a Japanese, born and raised in Japan, I have encountered many of the customs of Japanese religion even before my own birth! These experiences have provided an emic perspective as I conduct this study. I have drawn from a great deal of research in the fields of cultural anthropology, communication theory, ecclesiology, and Japanese culture and religion, as found in relevant precedent research literature and scholarly journals.

We are convinced that missiology starts from the context in which the Gospel communicates. The first step we take is to examine the Japanese worldview and culture in terms of cultural anthropology. The aim of this cultural analysis is to identify the questions raised from within the Japanese worldview.

Then we construct an ethno-ecclesiology for Japan. The procedure of ethno-ecclesiology construction can be divided into three dimensions. The first dimension refers to examining the Biblical data. Pauline ecclesiology provides a Biblical perspective on the Church and demonstrates how Paul formed and administered church structures according to the context of his congregations, and through this we can decode the essential function of the Church.

The second dimension deals with contemporary ecclesiology. Through this procedure, we expect to discover how contemporary Western theologians have contextualized the church to their context. Since any human perspective is limited and selective (only God views the whole picture of reality), contemporary ecclesiology provides a view of the church which is partial, but suggestive.

The third dimension refers integrating the Japanese context, the biblical data, and examples of contextualization from other contexts. We seek to answer questions emerging from the Japanese context, in conjunction with Pauline ecclesiology and in consultation with contemporary ecclesiology. Our intention is to identify some images and concepts of a Biblically sound church to which Japanese people can relate.

Finally, we suggest some possible recommendations for embodying those images/concepts of the Church. We examine the characteristics, approaches, tools, strategies and examples of a contextualized church based on the ethno-ecclesiology we have developed. We believe that a contextualized church serves both to make Christianity more relevant to the context of Japanese supernaturalism and to communicate New Testament concepts in Japan.

Chapter 2

Worldview Theory

The purpose of this chapter is to introduce the concept of worldview to provide a foundation for examining the Japanese cultural context. The worldview of a people is the way they look at reality. (Kearney, 1984:41) Since this worldview affects the way the message of Christianity is heard and interpreted, understanding worldview is a necessary basis for effective receptor-oriented communication. "It is the basis also for strategizing for presenting the Gospel as well as effectively nurturing the Christians." (M. Kraft in Grant 1985:385)

This chapter consists of six sections. First, I will discuss the issue of *perception* as the premise for the discussion of worldview. Second, I will explain the theoretical basis of worldview. Third, I will analyze the characteristics and the make-up of worldview. Fourth, I will describe the functions of worldview. Fifth, I will examine the idea of worldview universals. Finally, I will compare Japanese paradigms with Western and Hebrew worldviews.

2.1 Our Limited and Selective Perception

Before describing worldview theory, we need to account for the physical and social environment of the theory. Since worldview is a matter of perception, in this section we will examine how humans perceive reality.

Humans observe reality in a limited and biased way. Human perception is subject both to the limitations of our senses and the selectivity of our perceptions.

2.1.1 Our Limited Perception

Kraft likes to tell the well-known story of the blind men and the elephant to explain that our picture of the real world is always subjective, focused, limited and partial.

> Each blind man experienced a different part of the elephant and then generalized from that experience that the whole animal was like that part. One concluded that he was dealing with a hose, because the part he was holding—the trunk—seemed like a hose. Another concluded he was in contact with a tree-like being because he had grasped a leg. The others drew their conclusions from impressions of the elephant's tail, his side, his ear, or his tusks.
>
> And each was right when he concluded that this part of the elephant was like a tree, a wall, a hose, a rope, a fan, or a spear. But each was wrong when he generalized about the whole animal on the

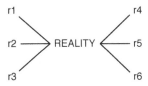

Figure 1: "Big R" Reality and "small r" reality (Kraft, 1987a:63)

> basis of his limited experience with but one part
> of the beast (1989:12–13).

In this story, there are two kinds of realities: One is objective reality, which exists outside the observers, symbolized in the story by the elephant. The other is subjective reality, which these blind men created in their minds. The blind men engaged a process of decoding in which their minds constructed their own models of reality through the grids of their biases. This decoding process has been illustrated by labelling the outside reality as "big R" Reality and the internalized reality as "small r" reality. (Kraft 1979:23f.; Kraft 1989:15f.)

Each observer has in his/her mind a "small r" reality, which is constructed on the basis of limited and partial understandings, provided by such things as our present and past experience, psychological makeup and sociocultural training. Although we cannot claim absolute understanding, we need to learn as much as possible about reality and to adjust our perception of reality accordingly. (Kraft, 1989:15)

Figure 2: Selecting Experiences (Hiebert, 1983a:5)

2.1.2 Our Selective Perception

The observer is not only limited but also highly selective in choosing his or her data. Hiebert introduces illustrations which show how the same scene might appear to three people in different situations in figure 2: left, to a young man "on the town"; center, to a person needing to cash a check; right, to someone late for an appointment.

The observer is really interested or concerned with only a few of the sense experiences with which he or she is bombarded. Obviously, the observer cannot react to or even interpret everything that appears in his field of vision, so those experiences that are irrelevant to the task at hand are either consciously or unconsciously screened out. In this way, the observer selectively perceives from the entire panorama data which is most relevant to his needs.

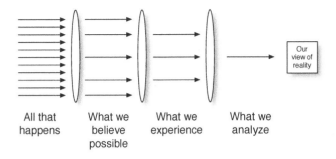

| All that happens | What we believe possible | What we experience | What we analyze |

Figure 3: Factors Influencing Our View of Reality (Kraft, 1989:19)

2.1.3   Like a Dim Image in a Mirror

In Corinthians 13:12, Paul points out that our view, unlike God's, is fuzzy and partial because of our humanity. "What we see now is like a dim image in a mirror; then we shall see face-to-face. What I know now is only partial; then it will be complete—as complete as God's knowledge of me." We see Reality through "lenses" or "filters". Kraft portrays some of these lenses in Figure 3.

The number of influences, which are indicated by the number of arrows, lessens as we go from one side of the chart to the other. There are, for example, a much greater number of things that happen than there are things we are taught to believe possible. The number of things that we eventually focus on to analyze and construct our view of reality is considerably less than the total of all that we believe or have experienced. (Kraft, 1989:19)

All human beings learn as children to see (big R) Reality in a particular way, which is why different people have different (small r) realities. We are looking at Reality in terms of a particular "grid" or mental map. This grid or mental map, or model, is built upon theories to which we unconsciously pledge allegiance without ever questioning them or even realizing their existence. (Kraft, 1987a:25) This grid or mental map limits what and how we understand.

2.2 Theoretical Basis

Many anthropologists have given valuable insights into the concept of *worldview*, but in my analysis I will mainly follow Kraft's model of worldview, consulting also models by Hiebert, Kearney and Opler.

Morris Opler developed the concept of *cultural themes*. He rejected Ruth Benedict's suggestion that cultures are dominated by a single integrative principle and offered his concept of themes which, as part of the worldview, unite the various cultural elements into an integrated whole. The state of equilibrium in a society is brought about by "counter themes" that act to restrain the extreme expression of a cultural theme. (Opler, 1946:201)

Michael Kearney repudiates the perspective of cultural idealism, and employs the perspective of historical materialism to construct a model of worldview. He uses the assumptions of "image" and "worldview" to refer to fundamental general perceptions and concepts of reality. "Taken together, the total of such primary images then constitute a worldview." (Kearney, 1984:47) Kearney postulates a dialectic model of worldview, which represents the dynamic interrelationship between the material environment, worldview, sociocultural behavior and a cultural symbol system. (1984:119f.) He suggests that the nature of the integration and interaction between units of worldview is both structural and logical, which leads him to coin the expression, "logico-structural integration." (1984:52f.) He also gives serious attention to the idea of "world-view universals," which are fundamental cognitive categories that can be found in any worldview as common elements. (1984:65–107)

For Paul Hiebert, one of the central motivating factors in the construction of a worldview model is the need to make life meaningful. Worldviews are constructed and reformulated in order to avoid the fear and cognitive anxiety created when a society's explanation system proves to be inadequate for constructing meanings and explanations for life's experiences. (Bensley, 1982:20)

> At the core of each culture, there seems to be certain basic assumptions about the natures of reality and morality. Many are implicit, because they are taken for granted and never questioned. Together, they form a more or less consistent world view that orders people's experiences and gives meaning to their lives. (Hiebert, 1983a:369)

Hiebert believes that it is useful to think of a worldview as having three dimensions: cognitive, expressive and evaluative. (1985:30–35; 1990:43) The cognitive dimension provides 1) various processes for creating categories, 2) frameworks which form the "existential assumptions" about what exists in the world, and 3) foundations for organizing the categories into larger models or pictures of reality. The expressive dimension includes feelings of gratification/deprivation, of wants/needs, of like/dislike and love/hate. The evaluative dimension provides the standards for making judgments and also determines the priorities and allegiances of the people. Taken together, these dimensions provide a society with a view of what the world is really like. The worldview serves as the foundation on which they construct their explicit belief and value systems, and the social institutions within which they live their daily life. (1985:47–48)

Charles Kraft's model of worldview is, similarly to Hiebert's, derived from the twin perspectives of cultural anthropology and Evangelical Christianity. In reality, both men display a great degree of commonality in terms of their theological frameworks and allegiances. Kraft's concern, however, is "how the systems work" and, from that, "how the systems change" from an etic perspective, while Hiebert's concern is primarily "what the systems mean" from the emic perspective.

When analyzing culture, Kraft distinguishes between surface-level behavior and deep-level assumptions. It is these assumptions which are called *worldview*. The cultural behavior is generated by people who are largely habitual but also creatively responsive to their worldview perception of reality. Kraft acknowledges people's potential to change their culture. People are pressed into a psycho-cultural mould, but there is within that mould some leeway, some space within which they have a degree of freedom of choice, what Kraft likes to call "room to wiggle." (Kraft, 1987a:173) We are 100% culturally *conditioned*, but not totally *determined*. This flexible approach to culture that is open to innovation has provided a good foundation for cross-cultural Christian communication.

2.3 Society's Map of Reality

A model or map of reality provides a patterning in terms of which we can chart our life's course. However, such patternings do not simply operate at the individual level. We are taught by those who raise us certain socially acceptable patterns concerning what to focus on and how to interpret things. (Kraft, 1989:19) Large numbers of people employ the same perception of the Reality around them. They are not only taught to view Reality in socially prescribed ways, but also are constantly pressured by other members of society to maintain those perspectives.

2.3.1 Definition of Worldview

Worldview is a perception shared by a social group. Kraft defines worldview as the culturally structured assumptions, values, and commitments underlying a people's perception of Reality. (Kraft, 1989:20)

2.3.2 Characteristics of Worldview

Kraft lists four characteristics of worldview in his *Anthropology Text*. (1987a:34f.)

1. Worldview assumptions are not reasoned out, but assumed to be true without prior proof. For example, the Japanese assume that the floor in the house (*tatami*) is clean, so they take off their shoes at the entrance of the house. The cleanness of the floor is assumed to be absolute, and is seldom questioned.

2. Worldview organizes people's lives and experiences into an explanatory whole they seldom—if ever—question, unless some if its assumptions become challenged by experiences that people cannot interpret. If the area in which people have lost confidence is considered by them to be very important, then the result can often be widespread demoralization within the society.

3. There are two basic types of worldview assumptions. One group of assumptions concerns the way things are. These assumptions are sometimes technically referred to as "cosmological" or "existential" postulates. (e.g., the unique absolute that God exists, or that such a God does not exist.) The other kind of assumption is labelled a "value." These assumptions provide the basis for judgments concerning what is good and what is not good. (e.g. harmony orientation versus individualistic competition.)

4. Of all the difficulties that occur in intercultural contact, those arising from differences in worldview are the most difficult to deal with. For example, when my wife arrived in California, her initial surprise was over the lack of security in American society. The complicated security systems required, with many keys and instructions, were of great concern to her. She grew up in Japan where crime rates are extremely low in spite of the highly developed industrialization and urbanization. It took a long time for her to accept the assumption that she needs make an effort to protect her life, family and property.

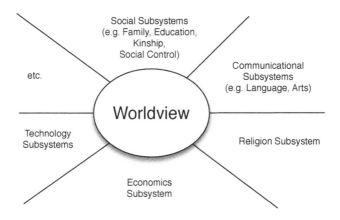

Figure 4: Internal Organization of Culture (Kraft, 1987a:130)

2.3.3 Ways of Looking at Worldview

There are various ways of looking at worldview.

Relationship to Culture

Worldview is the generator and integrator of the total cultural system. The various subsystems of culture radiate out from worldview. These are strongly interdependent, yet readily identifiable substructures.

Components of Cultural Subsystems

Each subsystem consists of the following characteristics: assumptions, rituals and creative behavior. It is portrayed as follows:

21

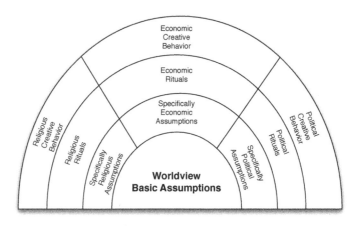

Figure 5: Make Up of Subsystems

The basic assumptions underlying all cultural subsystems constitute the worldview, yet each of the subsystems embodies additional assumptions specific to its own special sphere. (Kraft, 1987a:139) For example, the group orientation of the Japanese is one of the major, basic assumptions on the worldview level, and so individualistic approaches simply do not work, whether in religious groups, in business society, or in political relationships. There are, however, specifically *religious* assumptions within the religious subsystem levels, which concern appropriate symbols, rituals, institutions, modes of leadership, and the like. The principles of group-orientation, such as the stress on the parent-child relationship, have even been introduced into Japan's otherwise Westernized Christian churches. This assumption with regard to the leadership pattern of the church leader is a specifically religious assumption on the subsystem level, and should be distinguished from the assumptions founded on the worldview level. These assumptions are worked out in rituals (habitual behavior) and in creative behaviors specifically appropriate to each sphere of life.

Logico-Structural Integration

The basic assumptions that lie at the core of worldview are systematically interrelated. Kearney calls this structural integration of culture "logico-structural integration". He believes that the organization of worldview assumptions is shaped in two ways.

> The first of these is due to internal equilibrium dynamics among them. This means that some assumptions and the resultant ideas, beliefs, and actions predicated on them are logically and structurally more compatible than others, and that the entire world view will "strive" toward maximum logical and structural consistency. The second and main force giving coherence and shape to a world view is the necessity of having to relate to the external environment. In other words, human social behavior, social structure, institutions and customs are consistent with assumptions about the nature of the world. (1984:52)

Culture is an integrated organism, with each aspect interdependent upon each other. (Kraft, 1987a:140)

Conceptual Components

Other anthropologists, such as Ruth Benedict in *Patterns of Culture*, (1934) picture a worldview more wholistically, as the personality of a culture. Just as a human being manifests personality structure as an integrative component in his/her psychology, so too does a culture manifest a worldview. This view labels whole cultures in terms of a single dominant personality trait, which obviously cannot avoid oversimplification.

In response to Benedict's contention, Opler (1946) introduced the concept of "cultural themes." He recognized a greater complexity at the worldview level, and analyzed it in terms of a complex interaction between a dozen or more cultural themes. Opler defines a theme as a "position, declared or implied, and usually controlling behavior or stimulating activity, which is tacitly approved or openly promoted in a society." (1946:198) For example, Hiebert compares American cultural themes with Japanese cultural themes in table 1 on the facing page.

Kraft's framework for worldview is composed of three basic conceptual components, each of which lie at three different layers of conceptual complexity: themes, paradigms and models. (Kraft, 1987b:16–19) These components represent the more operational dimension of a worldview. Within the themes there are thousands of semi-independent perspectives that can be distinguished. They are images of smaller segments of reality that function as the operative segments of a worldview. Those perspectives are referred to as "paradigms." Within the paradigms there are many models, which are still smaller, less complex segments of reality. This analysis may depicted as in Figure 6 on the next page.

American Cultural Themes	Japanese Cultural Themes
Absolute	Relativistic
Natural/supernatural distinction	Wholistic
Categorization	Unity
Linear time	Cyclical time
Individualistic	Corporate orientation
Stress possessions	Stress relationships
Competitive	Cooperative
Sin/forgiveness	Defilement/purity
Nuclear family	Extended family
Stress spousal relationships	Stress parent-child
Immediate profit in business	Long range market share

Table 1: Comparison of Cultural Themes (Hiebert, 1990:42)

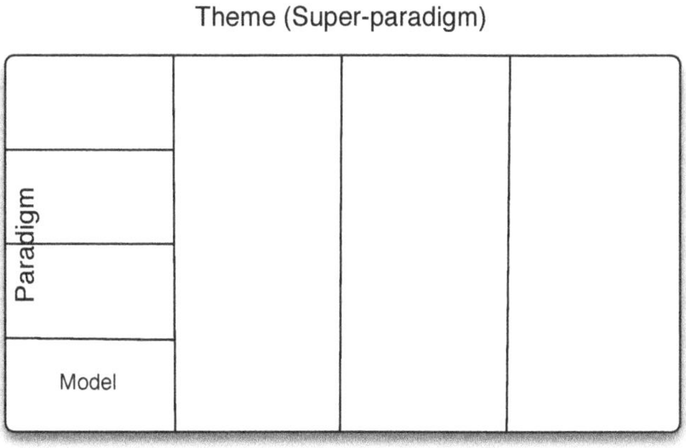

Theme (Super-paradigm)

Figure 6: Themes, Paradigms and Models

For example, we may refer to "supernatural orientation" as one Japanese cultural theme, "*kami*" (many deities who dispense life-giving power or destructive power) as one of the paradigms, and "*harai*" (purification rite) as one of the models.

2.4 Worldview Functions

There are many functions served by a worldview. Kraft highlights six of the most important in *Christianity with Power*. (1989:184f.; see also Kraft 1979:54–57, Kraft 1987a:41–46, Hiebert 1985:48–49.)

Worldview provides explanations for how things have got to be the way that they are and what keeps them that way. We develop our picture of what Reality looks like in terms of these explanatory assumptions. Assumptions underlying explanations concern every sphere of life and answer various questions as to the origin and nature of things, and are especially concerned those ultimate issues on which our lives are based. A common contrast in explanatory assumptions concerning the origin and nature of the universe is between those who believe the universe to be mechanistic, impersonal, and controllable by humans, and those who picture the universe as capricious and spirit-controlled.

2.4.1 Evaluating and Validating

A second function served by worldview is to enable people to evaluate what goes on around and inside of them. In the learning of a worldview, people are taught to evaluate the basic institutions, values and the goals of their society. They are taught a socially-approved structuring of the emotive or affective dimension of human life, which gives the impression that what is being done is valid or invalid, right or wrong, good or bad. They then commit themselves to what they highly value.

The Japanese people tend to offer flowers and incense sticks to the spirit of the departed at an intersection where a traffic fatality may have occurred. Such a supernatural-oriented action is valued positively because people have, as an unchallenged assumption, learned to consider it good. This kind of assumption serves as a kind of in-built mechanism to make judgments about what is good and what is not good, what is valid and what is not valid.

2.4.2 Assigning and Prioritizing Commitments

A third function of worldview is to enable us to sort out, arrange, and make different commitments, allegiances, and loyalties to the things we assume, value and do. We are taught to relate to each aspect of life with some degree of intensity, committing ourselves quite strongly to certain beliefs, values, and behaviors—but weakly or even indifferently to others.

Kraft makes an interesting illustration with regard to how people of different societies make the difficult choice between conflicting loyalties.

> A man, his mother, and his wife are crossing a river in a canoe when the canoe capsizes. Neither of the women can swim, the man is a weak swimmer, and the river is flowing swiftly. This means he can only rescue one of the women. If you were that man, which one would you rescue?

> In response, Anglo-Americans and northern Europeans tend to opt for rescuing the wife. Non-Westerners, southern Europeans, and Latin Americans, on the other hand, usually claim (often without hesitation) that they would rescue the mother. "You can always get another wife," they often reason, "but you can never replace a mother." In discussing this conundrum in class once, a Japanese student provided us with another option. He said, "I would just have to drown without rescuing either. I could neither make such a choice nor face my community afterwards if I allowed either of them to die." (1989:188–189)

This illustration points us the strong Japanese commitment to the community. Takeo Doi analyzes the relationship between "individual" and "group," and expresses this psychological desire to "belong" as *amae*. (1973:132–141; see Minami 1983:204.)

2.4.3 Interpreting

All of this prioritizing provides people with the structure they need to interpret and assign meaning to life. When society members attempt to interpret and assign meaning to their world, they find themselves guided in this process by the tracks of the worldviews they are taught.

Kraft has the impression that new habits of interpretation usually result from new allegiances and perspectives. (1989:191) For example, when a person pledges allegiance to

Jesus Christ, at least one major component of his or her view of Reality is changed.

There is a direct and close relationship between the interpretive conclusions we draw and the assumptions we start with. If our basic assumptions are to be truly Christian, we will automatically interpret and behave as God wants us to.

2.4.4 Integrating

A fifth function served by worldview is to push a culture and its people toward integration. It systematizes and orders people's perceptions of reality into an overall design. "Though no culture is perfectly integrated, all are integrated well enough that anything that is changed in one part of the culture automatically has ramifications for the rest of the culture." (Kraft, 1989:191–192)

Worldview functions as the nerve center of a culture—everything gets fed into it, and it also functions as the glue that holds things together.

> People with a common worldview tend to apply the same principles and values in all areas of life. If their worldview value in one area of life is individualism, they are likely to be individualistic in virtually all areas of life. Their life and culture are integrated around such a guiding principle. (Kraft, 1989:192)

2.4.5 Adapting

Worldview assumptions provide guidance when we perceive that things are not as we believe they ought to be. When other assumptions are challenged and we are forced to modify our perspectives in a given area of life, although the most frequent initial response is defensiveness, we may shift our perception of reality. When there is a certain amount of openness, or when the perception persists and we are unable to deny it, then we may choose to change some aspect of our worldview.

Sometimes the challenges are too great, or for some other reason people are unable to handle the pressures of modification. Then there may occur a breakdown at the worldview level, possibly resulting in demoralization (manifested in symptoms such as psychological, social, and moral breakdown) and, unless it is checked and reversed, in cultural disintegration.

"Worldview schizophrenia" is one way to adapt to such pressure. Persons and groups may even attempt to retain two sets of mutually contradictory assumptions, sometimes basing their behavior on one set of assumptions, sometimes on the other. Today the Japanese people may have parts of two worldviews competing within them: the traditional Japanese worldview and the Western worldview.

2.5 Worldview Universals

There are several categories of assumptions that seem to be found in every worldview, which Kearney terms "world-view universals." (Kearney, 1984:65f.) We largely follow Kraft's analysis of worldview universals. (1987a:39f.; 1989:195f. See also Hiebert 1990:46f.).

2.5.1 Categorization

Worldview provides a structure or pattern for the way people categorize or classify their perceptions of reality. People classify the reality they perceive around them: animals, people, things, material objects, social categories, natural and supernatural entities, the visible and the invisible. All are labeled and put into categories together with other items and entities believed to be similar to them.

A people's language provides the most obvious clue to their system of categorization. (Kraft, 1989:195) The Japanese people have been interested in natural phenomena, especially in their observation of rain, and have many categories to classify it that relate to the distinctive four seasons. For example, there are many linguistic forms which refer to "rain": early spring rain (*harusame*), early summer rain (*samidare*), the rainy season in June (*tsuyu*), an evening shower in summer (*yudachi*), the rainy season in autumn (*akisame*), a shower in late autumn and early winter (*shigure*).

2.5.2   Person/Group

Kraft labels the second area of worldview as 'person/group'. Worldview provides the way the human universe is perceived in both its internal and external relationships. It can be understood in the same way by all the members of a society.

The Japanese are taught to see people primarily as a group. In Japan it is important that control of the individual's feeling be subjugated to the group. A group often has priority over an individual, such that an individual will compromise his or her own values with the aim of benefitting the group to which he or she belongs. The Japanese usually follow the logic of the group and discount the logic of the individual. (Araki, 1973:53)

2.5.3   Causality

A third area of worldview is the matter of causality. The questions being answered under this label are such questions as: What causes things? What power lies behind such causation? What forces are at work in the universe? What results do they bring about? Are the forces personal, impersonal, or both? The answers are usually given in terms of God, gods, spirits, demons, luck, fate, karma, chance, cause and effect, political and economic structures, the power of persons, and so on.

The Japanese, for example, perform a rite of Shinto known as *jichinsai* before constructing a new building. *Jichinsai* is a ceremony for purifying a building site from the polluting spirits which occupy it. Even when the building is a super-modern high-technology building, they perform the same purification ritual. They invite a Shinto priest who is believed to be able to cast out evil spirits from the land, purifying it from pollution. The Japanese assume that evil spirits cause pollution in certain places and that humankind can, through these purification rites, bring about a spiritual change on the Earth.

2.5.4   Time/Event

All worldviews provide people with guidelines around times and events, conceptualizing daily, weekly, monthly, yearly, seasonally, and otherwise recurring events.

Frequently, a worldview focuses on the quality of an event rather than on the quantity of time consumed by that event. Such a worldview has an "event orientation" focus, as opposed to a "time orientation" worldview.

The traditional way of perceiving time for the Japanese people is cyclical. The stress of cyclical time is found in the repetition of events such as day and night, summer and winter, and the transmigration of the human life. There may be movement over time, but essentially the focus is on repeated experience. (Hiebert, 1990:46)

2.5.5 Space/Material

Worldview provides assumptions concerning space and the material world:

> Whether it is a matter of how to structure a building or how to arrange the space within a building; or whether it is a concern over how to conceive of and relate to certain features of the universe, or what value a society puts on material objects. The point is a people's worldview provides the rule. (Kraft, 1989:201)

Hall pictures an illustration that space communicates:

> In Latin America the interaction distance is much less than it is in the United States. Indeed, people cannot talk comfortably with one another unless they are very close to the distance that evokes either sexual or hostile feelings in North America. The result is that when they move close, we withdraw and back away. As a consequence, they think we are distant or cold, withdrawn and unfriendly. We, on the other

hand, are constantly accusing them of breathing down our necks, crowding us, and spraying our faces.

Americans who have spent some time in Latin America without learning these space considerations make other adaptations, like barricading themselves behind their desks, using chairs and typewriter tables to keep the Latin American at what is to us a comfortable distance. The result is that the Latin American may even climb over the obstacles until he has achieved a distance at which he can comfortably talk. (Hall in Grant 1985:108)

In Japan, the interaction distance is much more than it is in the United States, and therefore there may be even more difficulty when Japanese talk with people from Latin America.

Worldview is unconsciously formed in people's process of enculturation. They are not always consciously aware of their worldview even though these assumptions, values, and allegiances underlie their actions and give them meaning.

2.6 Paradigm Comparison

Though oversimplified, the following chart will help in understanding differences in basic assumptions between Western, Hebrew and Japanese people. It is based on Kraft's chart of "Western and Hebrew Paradigms". (1989:202–205)

Table 2: Comparative Paradigms

Western Paradigms	Hebrew Paradigms	Japanese Paradigms
Categorization, Classification, Logic		
a) Life is analyzed in neat categories.	a) Everything blurs into everything else.	a) Everything blurs into everything else.
b) Natural and supernatural dichotomy.	b) Supernatural affects everything.	b) Supernatural affects everything.
c) Clear difference between human, animal, and plant life.	c) Similar assumption.	c) Animistic.
d) Linear logic	d) Contextual logic	d) Contextual logic
Person/Group		
a) Individualism. Group interests are usually subservient to individual concerns. Important decisions are made by individuals of almost any age or status.	a) The group is the reality. Individual interests are usually subservient to group concerns. Important decisions are made as a group.	a) Corporatism. The mutual benefits between the group and individual is sought and harmony is the crucial element.
b) Equality of persons	b) Different persons are of different value, according to their status in the hierarchy.	b) Equality in the same social class.
c) Oriented toward freedom. Society is to provide as much freedom as possible for individuals.	c) Oriented toward security. Society is to provide as much security as possible for individuals.	c) Oriented toward material benefit and sense of belongingness.
d) Competition is good. (need to "get ahead")	d) Competition is evil. (need to "work together")	d) Schizophrenic shifts between values of competition and harmony.
e) The majority rules in a democracy.	e) Certain people are "born to rule".	e) Majority rules in a group logic.
f) Human-centered universe.	f) God and tribe/family-centered universe.	f) Spirits and company/family centered universe.

g) Money and material possessions are the measure of human value.	g) Family relationships are the measure of human value.	g) Company/family relationships are the measure of human value.
h) Biological life is sacred.	h) Social life is supremely important.	h) Tension between social and biological values.

Cause and Power

a) Incredible faith is shown in "chance." Cause and effect relationships are key and limit what can happen.	a) God causes everything.	a) Schizophrenic between spirits and chance.
b) Humans are in charge of nature through science.	b) God is in charge of everything.	b) Universe is autonomous.
c) Scientific strategy and technique will give humans total power over all things.	c) Strategy and technique in the spiritual realm is the source of whatever control we may achieve. Learning control via spiritual techniques is crucial.	c) Schizophrenic tension between Hebrew way and Western way.
d) Power over others is structured via business, politics and other organizations.	d) Power over others is structured by social patterns ordained by God.	d) Power over others is structured by economic patterns developed by higher social classes.
e) There are no invisible beings in the universe.	e) The universe is full of invisible beings who are very powerful.	e) The universe is full of invisible beings who give people life-giving power and destructive power.

Time and Event

36

a) Linear time is divided into neat segments. Each event in life has a new one.	a) Cyclical or spiraling time. Very similar events constantly recurring.	a) Cyclical time.
b) Oriented toward the near future.	b) Oriented toward the past.	b) Oriented toward the present.
c) "Time oriented." Events are scheduled according to the clock and calendar. We arrive at appointments at prearranged clock time.	c) "Event Oriented." Quality (not time) of event is crucial. The event starts when the proper people are present (not according to clock time).	c) "Time Oriented." Trust is developed by punctuality.
d) History is an attempt to objectively record "facts" from the past.	d) History is an attempt to preserve significant truths in a way meaningful today whether or not all details are objective facts.	d) History has meaning only when it justifies or supports today's actions.
e) Change is good. It is called "progress."	e) Change is bad. It means destruction of traditions.	e) Technical change is good, but value change is bad.
Space, The Material Sphere		
a) The universe evolved by chance.	a) The universe was created by God.	a) The concept of 'universe' is vague.
b) The universe can be dominated and controlled via science and technology.	b) The universe is to be responsibly managed by us as stewards of God.	b) Humans are a part of the universe.
c) The universe is like a machine.	c) The universe is more personal.	c) Schizophrenic between mechanical and personal.
d) Material goods are a measure of personal achievement.	d) Material goods are a measure of God's blessing.	d) Material goods are a measure of both personal achievement and spiritual blessing.

37

Part II

Japanese Worldview and Religious Rituals

Chapter 3

Japanese Supernaturalism and other Worldview Themes

When one analyzes the worldview paradigm of the Japanese, it is easy to identify a number of schizophrenic tendencies in respect of various worldview universals. On one hand, for instance, the Japanese live in a very advanced, Westernized, industrial society, and have learnt that humans can, through the use of scientific knowledge and instruments, exercise dominion over all things. On the other hand, though, they have a deeply rooted belief that spirits are at work in this world and the next world, and that humans can exercise dominion over everything through spiritual strategies and artifices. This tension between modernity and tradition is a major characteristic of modern Japanese.

This worldview schizophrenia is not unique to Japan. Many industrialized countries are rapidly plunging into the post-modern era. It is characterized by Naisbitt's megatrends of high technology, rapid culture change and the need for close human relationship. Naisbitt calls it 'post-industrial culture.' (1982) Computer science is bringing societies away from an industrial base, with a production orientation, toward one in which information is central. People in contemporary information societies may need to passively absorb a wealth of information, making it even more difficult for them to establish active self-sufficiency.

It is Inagaki's analysis that the post-modern condition is bringing about a parallel revival of interest in traditional religions. Individuals have become mere pawns in a technologically-advanced society, uncertain of their personal dignity. They are therefore drawn towards "irrational" religion as a reaction against contemporary rationalism. "This post-modern emptiness is now being filled by a vital religious revival, with one illustration being the boom of occult religion among young people in Japan." (Inagaki, 1990a:8)

Inagaki modifies Shaeffer's dichotomy diagram, (1976:163) seeing an upper stratum of rationalism transplanted from the West which is not indigenous to non-Western cultural spheres such as Japan. The lower tier is the traditional Japanese worldview, which has a spiritual, supernatural orientation. He calls it "Japanism," emphasizing the worldly character of the Japanese; however, we will call it "Japanese supernaturalism," emphasizing its supernatural orientation. Hayashi constructs a similar diagram and shows that the surface layer, which is a compromise of the so-called "scientific and modern" worldview, is narrower in comparison to the underlying traditional layer. (Hayashi, 1988) Hayashi's diagram expresses

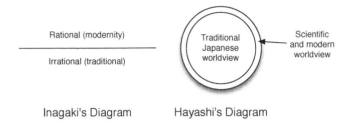

| Rational (modernity) | | Scientific |
| Irrational (traditional) | Traditional Japanese worldview | and modern worldview |

Inagaki's Diagram   Hayashi's Diagram

Figure 7: The Double Layer Structure of the Japanese Worldview

more than Inagaki's the supremacy of the traditional within Japanese worldview. (See figure 7.)

Nishiyama calls the nature of the ancient religion in Japan "spiritual manipulation," and insists that this pragmatic, mystical, shamanistic religiosity has worn different clothes and emerged repeatedly in history like a dress-up doll.[1] (Nishiyama, 1984) Today's new and folk religions are in a sense a revival of ancient Japanese religious concepts presented in the new context of contemporary Japan, and especially the context of urban life, or within a contemporary cosmological framework. This old-yet-new worldview is the subject of this chapter.

Japanese supernaturalism is a part of the traditional magico-religious worldview. It is one of the major worldview themes which has lain at the bottom layer of the Japanese worldview and actively influenced the whole of Japanese culture.

It is crucial to investigate Japanese supernaturalism in order to understand Japanese culture. It is the *basso osti-*

[1] Ishida (1983) expresses the same idea by the term "function-ism."

43

nato, in Maruyama's terminology. (Shukyo-shakaigaku-no-kai, 1985:iv) The aim of this chapter is to investigate the predominant position of Japanese supernaturalism within Japanese culture by analysing the its relationship to other worldview themes.

3.1 Unity of Japanese Religion (Syncretism)

Japanese religion is generally recognized to include the following religious traditions: the formal religions of Shinto, Buddhism, Christianity, and numerous New Religions; the less formal traditions of Confucianism and Taoism; and the practices and beliefs of folk religion. These traditions coexist in Japan.

This is not to say that in some areas people believe in *kami* (Shinto deities), while in other areas people believe in the Buddha. An assimilative tendency in Japanese society and a history of adaptation has given rise to the complex, multiform Japanese religious phenomena. As Gorai (1986:164) points out, in Japan's case, unlike in that of other societies, ancient religious traditions have remained steadfast despite the introduction of Buddhism, Confucianism, Taoism, and Christianity. Through the process of contact and exchange between other cultures and the faith, rituals and practices of the indigenous Shinto religion, many of the borrowed ethical and religious elements have been fused with Japanese religions, reinterpreted, and resystematized into Japanese religion.

> They intermingled so completely that they lost
> their individual identities, and they have actu-

ally played the traditional roles of state religion and/or family religion. Confucianism and
Shinto have borrowed Buddhist metaphysics
and psychology; Buddhism and Shinto have
borrowed many aspects of Confucian theory
and ethics; and Confucianism and Buddhism
have adapted themselves rather thoroughly to
the indigenous religion of Japan instead of
maintaining their particularity, though of course
their manifestations are many and varied. (Hori,
1968:10)

Japanese religion cannot be understood simply by separating it into individual components. It does not go too
far to say that the names 'Shinto' and 'Buddhism' and so
on express different facets of a single, syncretized Japanese
religion. Murayama points out the misunderstanding the
Japanese themselves have:

Many Japanese hold to the conception that
Shinto is indigenous and Buddhism is imported,
but before Shinto came into contact with Buddhism it had already been influenced by Chinese Taoism, while Buddhism itself had also
undergone a process of Sinification, becoming
confused with Chinese thought before being
introduced into Japan. Therefore the confusion
of Shinto and Buddhism was not just the mixing
of the two religions, nor the simple tangle of
national and foreign. (Murayama, 1990:2)

What stands out in this assimilative process is not friction
or disharmony in the value systems but the continuity and

harmony. The Japanese Ministry of Culture suggests that one factor contributing to this cultural characteristic is Japan's geographical situation.

> A relatively small country completely surrounded by the sea, Japan has maintained close contacts with China since ancient times, for her geographical position favored her receiving and assimilating cultural influences from the mainland. She was close enough to China to accept Chinese cultural influences, yet far enough away to be relatively safe from military invasion and the political control of the overwhelmingly powerful Chinese dynasties. (Japan Ministry of Culture, 1972:12)

They conclude that because of Japan's great distance from conquering nations, the imported elements never engulfed the existing ones. For this reason, Japan has been able to preserve a relatively continuous cultural identity from ancient times to the present.

Japanese religion cannot be understood simply by separating it into individual components, because Japanese people do not "belong" exclusively to just one religion. Several traditions may be combined in one religious activity, or a person may resort to one tradition for one purpose and then rely on another tradition for another purpose. (Earhart, 1984:22) Miyake describes the Japanese attitude toward religions as follows: "The Japanese may pray at the *kamidana* and *butsudan*, go to the shrine at New Year, the temple at *o-bon*, the church at Christmas, and then during a life crisis may go to a new religious group." (1974:89, in Reader 1991:51)

3.2 Groupism

Another element that Western modernism has introduced into Japan was individualism. The conflict between traditional groupism and contemporary individualism contributes to this current Japanese schizophrenia.

In Japan it is important to control individual emotion for the sake of the group. The group often asserts priority over an individual, with that individual conforming to the aim or the benefit of the group to which he belongs. In return, the group must give warmth and security, and meet the need of dependency of its members. The Japanese usually follow the logic of the group and suppress the logic of the individual. (Araki, 1973:53)

> Group consciousness is many things, including the principle of giving primacy to group goals no matter who is right in the event of different aims between an individual and the group, emotional attachment to acting communally with one's fellows, loyalty to the group or to a special individual who symbolizes the whole group and group pressure put on the individual to conform. (Kato, 1987:87)

This tendency has been nurtured in rice-producing fields in remote small communities divided by steep mountains. People have been united in close cooperation and organized into a closed human nexus, like a family. Rice production demands not only great manpower in a small field, but also cooperation, which transcends the individual and family units.

Agrarian	Pastoral
Stationary	Nomadic
Communalistic	Individualistic
Heteronomous	Autonomous
Group logic	Individual logic
Feminine	Masculine

Table 4: Agrarian versus pastoral cultures (taken from Araki 1973:23)

And there, in an emotional atmosphere that does not allow for individual claims, they have formed an understanding and a form of expression for getting along with each other. Table 4 compares the general characteristics of an agriculture-based culture with that of a cattle breeder's culture. It shows that group orientation is central to an agriculture-based culture.

Hamaguchi, however, points out that the methodology of the individualism-groupism antithesis is not useful when analyzing Japanese groupism. He calls the Japanese group orientation "corporativism," which seeks mutual benefit between the group and the individual and where harmony is the crucial element. He also recognizes the Japanese as a typical "referential subject" people and the Westerners as an "individual subject" people.

> If one evaluates someone at the *individual* level, they may be lacking in subjectivity in terms of their specialisms or authority. But they will have sufficient awareness of the work allotted to them in the workplace (in other words, their duty) and they will be extraordinarily diligent in achieving

48

it. They will also work with the understanding that everybody is a manager, paying attention to everything that happens in workplace, balancing the relationships between co-workers as well as other interested parties, in order to raise the level of cooperation for everyone. If one thinks about it from this perspective, it would be fair to say that the Japanese have subjectivity at a *group* level. (Hamaguchi, 1982:20–21)

The Japanese do not intend to sacrifice their desires and well-being to their group for the sake of the group's aims, but instead this is the method used to attain symbiosis with the group that they have commited themselves to. Many Westerners misunderstand the strong Japanese commitment to the company as a pure loyalty based on a Confucian ethical background. Yet most often, when they show fidelity to a group, they expect individual benefit in return. (See Muramatsu 1992:139–140.)

Why do the Japanese attach such great importance to relationships within the group? It seems to relate to their sense of belonging. The Japanese worldview is so "this-worldly," not allowing for the existence of an absolute value beyond the interests of the group to which a person belongs, that the individual simply accepts the group or makes it the framework for acting and living. In this way group consciousness is strengthened and an identity established for them. Ogata illustrates the Japanese need for belongingness:

A Japanese employee has a feeling of belongingness to his company. The employees tend to totally commit themselves to their company.

49

> Japanese students, too, have a conscious belong-
> ingness to their schools. In the villages of Japan,
> each family has a feeling of belonging to its
> village, so if a family becomes Christian and
> refuses to attend the village's Shinto festival,
> the village people rebuke the family. In Japan,
> we see the people's feeling of belongingness to
> the nation. Generally, most Japanese people are
> proud of the Japanese race. (1985:44)

This sense of belongingness has given the Japanese their predilection towards group orientation. Moreover, it has produced a fear of the breakdown of human relationships. Many Japanese activities can be explained by the following fundamental proposition: *Japanese people have a latent phobia of isolation.* Minami calls the source of this anxiety "a sense of self-uncertainty" which is dispelled—or at least, alleviated—by casting oneself upon the group, or on fate. (Minami, 1983:10–12) Japanese people have a fear of death, but much greater than death, they have a fear of ostracism (*murahachibu*).

Doi (1973) uses the concept of *amae* (variously translated as 'dependence' or 'selfish love') to analyse attitudes which affirm dependence, and portrays this as the fundamental element in Japanese interpersonal relationships. *Amae* is related to the psychology of a never-fully-satisfied desire to be loved.

> The *amae* mentality could be defined as the at-
> tempt to deny the fact of human separation and
> to obliterate the pain of separation in personal
> relations. *Amae* in adults seeks, unrealistically, to

50

> maintain a kind of womb-like existence of warm,
> all-embracing, dependent relationships with oth-
> ers, even when reality demands independent
> standing alone. (Dale, 1977:155)

The denial of separation, or to put it another way, the infant's desire to be at one with its mother, makes the Japanese group-oriented.

Japanese supernaturalism has at least three functions relating to groupism. First, it is a projection onto the spiritual stage of the deep-seated need for *amae* which is not fulfilled by human relationships. The most common representation of this is in the devotion to the goddess of mercy Kannon (*Avalokiteshvara*), who will be especially familiar to the Japanese and recognized by them as symbolic of Shinto-Buddhism fusion. (Murayama, 1990:41–68) Kannon is benevolent and, like a mother indulging her child, desires to promptly and consistently grant any prayer, however selfish it may be. (Spiro, 1984) The maternal, nurturing characteristic of the Japanese gods has been pointed out by many scholars as a further example of this.

Second, Japanese supernaturalism provides an opportunity for the release of individual, internal emotions which are repressed by the heavy bonds of society. Ian Reader calls this useful emotional release mechanism the "catharsis function" of religion. "By acting out feelings and emotions and externalizing those inner desires, fears and worries, Japanese people have a channel through which they can therapeutically liberate those feelings and get them out in the open rather than bottling them up." (1991:187)

The third function of the Japanese supernaturalism in conjunction with the groupism is to help to channel what may

51

be personally beneficial and self-aggrandizing wishes into a legitimate framework. Prayer for success creates an element of competition in Japanese society. Ironically, however, Japanese society likes to stress the ideals of harmony and conformity to group norms. The apparent contradictions between the ethics of competition and conformity may be harmonized by placing one's fate into the hands of the gods. The socially desirable pursuit of success may be rationalized so as not to clash with the prevailing images of harmony that are widely promoted as social ideals in Japan.

3.3 Contextual logic (the non-existence of the absolute)

Another worldview theme we should discuss along with groupism is that of contextual logic. The Japanese maintain and strengthen relationships between individuals, and, in a sense, this can almost be said to be a sacred goal for the Japanese. They attach great value to relationships and mutual interdependence. The Japanese evaluate information on the basis of its relational context, and therefore it is very important to understand this contextual logic in order to communicate effectively.

This contextual logic orientation of Japanese has occurred from their predilection toward naively accepting the environment they have been given to live in. (See Nakamura 1989:13.) Many Japanese do not by any means recognise the existence of an absolute state isolated from environmental phenomena because, according to them, the phenomenal environment, whether made up of things visible or invisible, is itself the absolute.

> To the ancient Japanese people, however, this small land was the only world they knew and experienced. No doubt, the natural beauty, which is enhanced by seasonal change, nurtured the people's belief that Japan is a sacred land and is permeated by numerous kami, or divine spirits. Unlike many Westerners who feel that this world is a fallen world, the early Japanese took it for granted that the natural world was the original world, and they did not look for another order of meaning behind or beyond the natural world. (Kitagawa, 1987:274–275)

It is difficult for Japanese to accept the "absolutely inviolable sacred law of God." Japanese have little concern for the transcendent event, unless it is over the will of transcendent beings. There is no unique, absolute God, nor unchangeable institution. The only thing they can have faith in is the opinions of influential people, and in many cases, the opinion of the majority.

The Japanese sense of justice or ethics is also relativistic. As opposed to a divine canonical teaching, people's words and promises can easily change. When the will of a group changes, the standard behavior or the value of the group members may change paradoxically over a short period of time. Japanese call "justice" whatever is of benefit to the majority. That is why Isaiah Ben-Dasan, who expresses the Japanese mental structure as "Nihon-kyo", writes, "the fundamental principle of Nihon-kyo is the person. Accordingly, there is no theology, only human-ology." (1970:104).

"Harmony" is the key word in Japan, with a strong emphasis on the avoidance of conflict. Lack of absolute logic leads the Japanese to pursue symbiotic solutions together with the group, and so the Japanese mind, which does not recognize absolute justice authorized by an absolute God, wavers unsteadily. This leads to a tendency to harmonize oneself with others, and to adhere closely to the group. Japanese people want to avoid divisiveness and alienation.

Looking at the attitudes of the people and the results of the entrance of a foreign culture, including its religions, one will clearly understand the degree to which Japanese people will avoid things which could breach social harmony.

> Japanese culture has absorbed each successive sweep of incoming foreign cultures with a voracious appetite, but those parts of foreign culture which are essentially not suitable have been excreted right out again, or, on the other hand, have been so completely digested that they lose their own essential characteristics. (Mita, 1965:164)

This process of absorption becomes clear when one understands the characteristics of ancient Shinto. Primal Shinto has no canon, no teachings and no principles; or, to put it another way, it does not have any absolute religious values.

> It is no easy task to write intelligently on Shinto, particularly in the categories of Western thought. Shinto has no founder, no sacred scriptures, no established dogmas, and authentic interpreters. There is not even a uniform answer to the question whether Shinto is a "religion," or an ethic, or merely a style of life, typical of Japan. (Spae, 1971:17)

The Japan Ministry of Culture calls early Shinto "Basic Shinto," and identifies it with the fundamental value orientation of the Japanese people. (1972:29) Basic Shinto was an unorganized, undifferentiated and unnamed complex of animism, including nature worship, ancestor veneration, shamanism and agricultural cult. It could coexist with other introduced religions because of its lack of absolute values. The major trait of this religion is that it has retained the basic framework of an ethnic religion for a small community in spite of its syncretic development over a long period of time. The influence of Shinto has permeated the whole of ethnic history.

> It may be said that the value pattern underlying ancient Japanese culture and religion was characterized by a sense of continuity between *kami* and man, by its affirmation of human nature as essentially good and pure, and by its positive this-worldly orientation. This idea of absolute transcendence or negation of this-worldly values is conspicuously absent. It may be that the nonexistence of such ideas is characteristic of the archaic, ethnic religions of the world, but what is particularly striking about Japan is that this basic value pattern has survived, with modifications, to the present day. (Japan Ministry of Culture, 1972:16)

The Japanese have adapted to foreign cultural influences by exercising contextual logic, maintaining the fundamental framework of the Basic Shinto to the present time. One example may be seen in the sophistic policy of Prince Shotoku

(574–622), who marked the first major step in the development of Japanese Buddhism. This is called *shinbutsuju shugo* (a harmonious fusion of Buddhism, Shinto, and Confucianism).

> The Prince produced the following piece of sophistic logic: 'Spread the branches of Buddhism on the trunk of Shinto, let the decorums of Confucianism grow, and see material prosperity achieved,' asserting that adding one does not mean denying the others. (Sakaiya, 1991:140)

The relationships between human beings and innumerable deities and spirits have also been cultivated by contextual logic. There is no absolute covenant between human beings and the deities and/or spirits. People have appealed to spiritual beings for this-worldly benefits, such as the surmounting of illnesses, or the achievement of success, peace of mind and happiness. This relationship is not consistent. The religious world provides a psychological support system in times of need, to be called upon when circumstances require it, to provide answers and solutions when problems arise, and which, at other times, does not require attention. Situations lead people into religious behavior and into a relationship with gods. A popular Japanese saying is *komatta toki no kamidanomi*, "turn to the gods in times of trouble."

3.4   Life Cycle and Ancestor Veneration

The natural beauty of Japan's islands is largely due to the distinct seasonal climatic differences. There are clear distinctions among the four seasons. It is natural for the Japanese to think

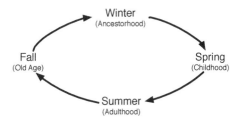

Figure 8: Japanese Time

of human life as a cycle, because they live in a cyclical seasonal change zone. Social life is segmented into seasons such as childhood, adulthood, old age and ancestorhood. Childhood corresponds to spring, adulthood to summer, old age to fall, ancestorhood to winter. (See Figure 8.) A 1983 survey by NHK[2] entitled "Japanese Religious Consciousness" proves that this paradigm has survived until the post-industrial age: 59% of the respondents answered "Yes" to the question, "Do you feel deep connections with your ancestors?"

The life cycle traverses its way through the two domains which constitute the cosmos:

> The first domain is the seen/empirical world in which we presently live. This domain is often referred to as *kono yo* (this world), *gense* (present age) or *busshitsukai* (the material world). The second domain is the unseen/transempirical world, usually referred to as *ano yo* (that world), *takai* (other domain), or *reikai* (the spirit world). It is thought that humans enter into this second

[2]One of the major broadcasting networks in Japan.

57

> domain when their spirit departs from their
> body at death. This is the domain in which
> ancestors, spirits, gods, goddesses, and ghosts are
> thought to reside. (Hayashi, 1988:182)

There are active interactions within the framework of these two domains. The boundary between the two domains is quite fuzzy. Spirits and deities in 'that world' can freely visit 'this world', interfering with or influencing events in this world.

Since the Japanese believe in the dual nature of humankind as well as immortality of the spirit, when a person dies, the spirit leaves the body and goes to another world while the flesh perishes. The ancestral spirit comes back to this world after completing a certain process. In short, humankind and gods exist on the same continuum, and there is no clearcut boundary between them as there is between God and humanity in Christianity. (See Figure 9 on the next page.)

This divine-human continuum is seen not only in ancestor veneration but also in shamanism, with its features of demon possession and soul release. It plays the major role in traditional Japanese religion as well as in new religions today. The divine-human continuum is a primary characteristic Japanese worldview theme.

In addition, the Japanese lack the concept of a self-existent, absolute God. The concept of a creator God who is independent of all things is absent in the Japanese worldview. Hayashi analyzes the Japanese perception of the cosmos based on Hiebert's analytical model (Hiebert, 1982) and concludes that while the middle level of the supernatural yet this-worldly beings is excluded from a Western two-tiered view of reality, the upper zone, the world of transcendence is either missing

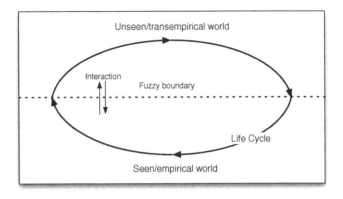

Figure 9: Japanese View of the Cosmos

or largely absent from a traditional Japanese worldview. (See figure 10 on the following page, and figures 11 and 12 on page 61.) "The Japanese concept of spiritual space is basically two-tiered, and it is strongly middle-zone-oriented." (Hayashi, 1988:185)

Therefore, Westernized theology, which reflects the Western worldview with its 'excluded middle', cannot meet the power-oriented needs of the Japanese people.

As stated above, the Japanese do not have a clear-cut dichotomy between humans and deity. Although the flesh will perish, the spirit (*tama*) of humankind lives eternally. For the spirit, therefore, death means transition to a different stage—ancestorhood—on the same continuum. The living spirit is called *ikimitama* or *ikiryo*, while the spirit of the deceased is called a *shiryo* and is spiritually powerful.

The *shiryo*, the spirit of the deceased, gradually diminishes in its spiritual might and rises in rank from *shiryo* to *hotoke* and

59

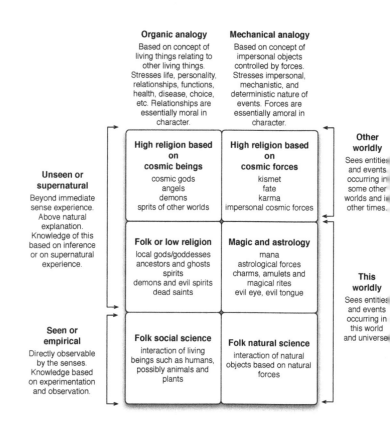

Organic analogy
Based on concept of living things relating to other living things. Stresses life, personality, relationships, functions, health, disease, choice, etc. Relationships are essentially moral in character.

Mechanical analogy
Based on concept of impersonal objects controlled by forces. Stresses impersonal, mechanistic, and deterministic nature of events. Forces are essentially amoral in character.

Unseen or supernatural
Beyond immediate sense experience. Above natural explanation. Knowledge of this based on inference or on supernatural experience.

High religion based on cosmic beings
cosmic gods
angels
demons
sprits of other worlds

High religion based on cosmic forces
kismet
fate
karma
impersonal cosmic forces

Other worldly
Sees entities and events occurring in some other worlds and in other times.

Folk or low religion
local gods/goddesses
ancestors and ghosts
spirits
demons and evil spirits
dead saints

Magic and astrology
mana
astrological forces
charms, amulets and magical rites
evil eye, evil tongue

This worldly
Sees entities and events occurring in this world and universe

Seen or empirical
Directly observable by the senses. Knowledge based on experimentation and observation.

Folk social science
interaction of living beings such as humans, possibly animals and plants

Folk natural science
interaction of natural objects based on natural forces

Figure 10: An Analytical Framework for the Analysis of a Religious System (Hiebert, 1982:40)

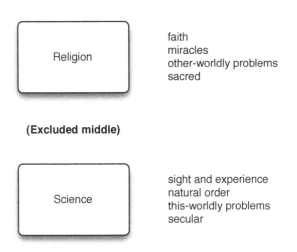

(Excluded middle)

Religion — faith, miracles, other-worldly problems, sacred

Science — sight and experience, natural order, this-worldly problems, secular

Figure 11: A Western Two-Tiered View of Reality (Hiebert, 1982:44)

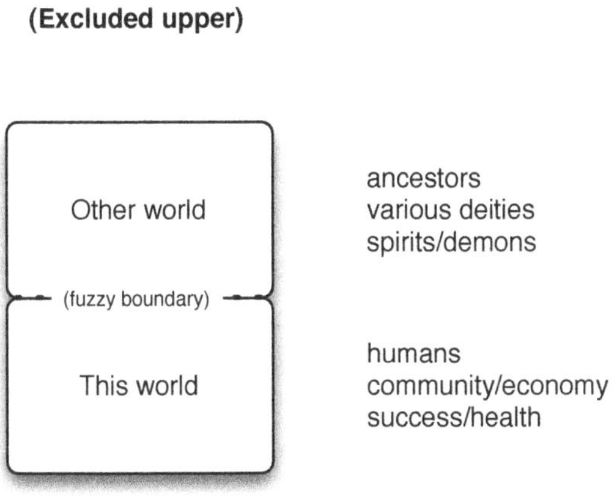

(Excluded upper)

Other world — ancestors, various deities, spirits/demons

(fuzzy boundary)

This world — humans, community/economy, success/health

Figure 12: A Japanese Two-Tiered View of Reality

then to *kami* through the repetition of ancestoral veneration rites practiced by the descendants. The *kami* is the ancestral spirit, brought about by close relatives sincerely carrying out religious rituals.

These ancestral spirits live near their home town and return at *o-bon*, a lantern festival, and on New Year's day. They are believed to bring abundant harvests and well-being to the people, and they are believed to reincarnate. (See Akata 1986:33.)

In this process where the *shiryo* (the spirit of the deceased) grows up to become a *kami* (ancestral spirit), people systematically hold a process of ancestor veneration rites for the dead, such as the seven-day rite, one-year rite, three-year rite, seven-year rite, 13-year rite, 17-year rite, 25-year rite and 33-year rite. Hisakazu Inagaki compares this process with the growth of a new born baby:

> When a *shiryo* is born [into the other world], they are given a posthumous name, just like babies are given their name. During the first month after birth, both of them experience a period of instability, a kind of period of pollution. When the month ends, both of them enter a process of purification and begin growing up by passing through the *ie* [familial] rites: the anniversary of their death, their gala day for children who are three, five and seven years old, and initiation rites. The rite for ending the condolatory period is held in the 33rd year, just as babies grow up and reach the age of marriage of around 33 years old and form a new

ie. [family] Thus, there is an analogy between the process of becoming an ancestor and becoming an adult. We can see birth-death-rebirth as the process of the "circulation of spirits." (Inagaki, 1990b:54–55)

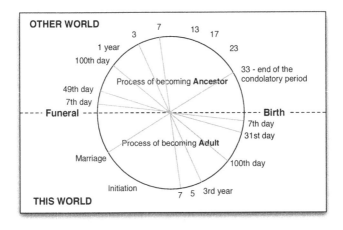

Figure 13: Circulation of the Human Spirit (Adapted from Inagaki 1990b:54)

The circulation of the human spirit is one of the major Japanese worldview themes, and this theme has originated from indigenous Shinto. However, since the introduction of Buddhism, the rites of passage concerned with the process of becoming an ancestor have been taken over by Buddhism because, according to Shinto ideas, death is considered pollution and the treatment of the dead body is taboo. Japanese people consider religious practices not only as an expression of inner allegiance but also as rites of passage. The Japanese people use religious activities functionally in their life cycle. (Hayashi and Yonezawa, 1982:96) Shinto handles the rites related to joy and harvest, and Buddhism handles the rites related to death and ancestor veneration, (Ohara, 1979:95) as can be seen in Figure 13 on the preceding page.

Yoshino (1982) claims that the ancient serpent cult has continued to this day, providing the basic framework for the Japanese worldview. This idea is persuasive in several ways: in particular, the concept of circulation of the human spirit; the interactions between this world (the human world) and the ancestral world (the serpent world) brought about through various religious practices; the idea of the other-world as the origin of life and death; and the worship of life-giving power. The most interesting indication is related to the existence of the Great Serpent who dominates both this world and the other world. He should be recognized as the symbol of life-giving energy, and this kind of belief system is observed within contemporary Japanese religiosity.

Two points should be made regarding the relation between Japanese supernaturalism and ancestor veneration. First, the cosmological sense of unity, expressed both by the circulation of the human spirit and by active interaction between the humans of this world and gods of the other world, is mirrored in the ways that religious themes also help to provide unity and coherence in social terms. This unity has provided, and has been used to provide, a sense of social cohesion, continuity, community and identity on many levels, from local and familial to regional and national.

> The Japanese are 'born Shinto and die Buddhist',
> thus incorporating both traditions into theirs,

> and their families' lives. This cyclical process emphasizes the importance of continuity and regeneration and indicates the vital role of the household as a continuing religious entity in its own right, central both to the individuals in it and to the continuity of the Shinto and Buddhist traditions. (Reader, 1991:56)

Because of the close ties on many levels between religious and social entities, Japanese culture provides people with both a spiritual connection and a strong sense of belonging to a group. Ancestor veneration is a set of symbolic rituals performed to unite an individual to his or her family, while, for the member of the group, it situates them in terms of both the society and the cosmos. In other words, Japanese have closely integrated two sources, the human world and the spiritual world, which together go towards maintaining their identity.

The second point is related to the spiritual influence of the *shiryo* (the spirit of the deceased) and the *kami* or *hotoke* (the ancestral spirit). The ancestors are believed to look over the living members of the family line. Ideally, the fact of separation of the spiritual life-giving force from the physical realm in which it exists can be transformed to the benefit of the living. The souls of the dead continue to feel benevolence towards the living and assist the process of renewal and continued prosperity through their benevolent guidance on the spiritual level. However, it is difficult for people in contemporary Japan, where not only the extended family but also nuclear family ties are breaking down, to acknowledge the ancestors as a *shugoshin* (guardian deity). Rather, the ancestral veneration rites have come to be presented as an explanatory system for crisis; they explain that sickness, the disintegration of the family, and various misfortunes all arise as a punishment by the ancestors for the lack of memorial services. One of the major elements of Japanese supernaturalism is the idea that ancestors, undergoing spiritual circulation in the other world, are active and influential, whether that influence be benevolent or malevolent.

3.5   Form Consciousness

Starting from the presupposition that Japanese are characterized by having a sense of self-uncertainty at the motivational base of their social behavior, Minami develops the motif of form consciousness. He asserts that the Japanese try to alleviate their uncertain sense of selfhood by attaching great importance to etiquette, ceremony and other fixed forms of behavior within everyday life. (1983:14–51)

Form consciousness can be found in various areas of Japanese life. Japanese are sensitive to the latest trends and fashions in leisure and sports, so their recreational activities are highly standardized and uniform. *Joseki* (formulae or established tactics) have been formed in *budo* (martial arts), *sado* (tea ceremony), *kado* (flower arrangement), *shogi* (Japanese chess), and *yomikaki-soroban* (education of reading, writing and abacus). Unconventional ways of study and mastery or self-taught methods of achievement have generally been shunned. Although form consciousness oppresses people's creativity and individuality, Sakaiya (1991:277–278) suggests that it relates to the establishment of a post-war industrialized society, heavily influenced by mass production of standard products.

Japanese religions are extremely ritual-oriented. As stated above, Shinto has no founder, no sacred scriptures, no established dogmas, nor authentic interpreters, but it has numerous molded styles of rituals. These include *shichi-go-san* (special family festivities for children on their third, fifth, and seventh birthdays) as well as *muneageshiki* (traditional roof beam-raising rituals) performed even for modern buildings under construction. Lack of contextual ritualization in Protestantism can be seen as one of the major reasons for the church's stagnation in Japan. Correctly following examples of strict and repetitively-patterned rituals are crucial for performing them. It is believed that *kami* require the strict observation of rituals so that they may be respected or find solace.

3.6 Self-surrender

Takeda (1987) acknowledges that strong traces of ancient irrational shamanism and the traditional exclusivistic collectivism remain in the ethos of the modern Japanese. She, however, thinks that if one too easily draws the conclusion that the Japanese do not aspire to or yearn for that which is transcendental and universal, then one will fail to grasp an extremely important part of Japanese culture. She stresses that the Japanese people have archetypes embedded deep within their collective unconscious.

> Japanese culture contains, at its deepest levels, not only elements such as irrational shamanism and exclusivistic collectivism, but also elements that aspire to or long for transcendental and universal value. (1987:172)

At the worldview or the deeper personal level, one may discover a motif in which Japanese aspire to transcendence by denying the ego-centered self. Inazo Nitobe published a work in English entitled *Bushido: the Soul of Japan* (1899) and summed up the moral and religious qualities of the Japanese people as a whole. He took *gi* (rectitude or justice), *yu* (courage), *jin* (benevolence), *rei* (politeness), *makoto* (veracity and sincerity), *meiyo* (honor), *chugi* (loyalty) and *kokki* (self-control) as Japanese moral values. It is true to say that most Japanese are similarly view Bushido as one ideal way of life. (Katsube, 1987:44)

This is different from the Western concept of an ethical law, because Japanese are far from the concept of keeping a covenant with an absolute God. Japanese grasp this ideal as an aesthetic image. When faced with the purity inherent within self-denial, they feel this concept of covenant is "beautiful" rather than necessarily evaluating it as "good."

A covenant of self-denial is easily interpreted, whether consciously or unconsciously, as the way to attain mystical unity with divine beings. (Morimoto, 1991:273) Kajimura (1988) presents the insightful thesis that the ideal way of life is seen as surrendering oneself and leaving a matter to follow its natural course. He quotes Shinran, the founder of a Pure Land Buddhist sect, and introduces the concept of *shizen* ('nature'). Shinran explains the figure and nature of Buddha by saying that the Buddha has an enormous body which fills the heavens and the earth, and enormous hands which stretch out to embrace all living things. However, Shinran teaches that this explanation of the Buddha is a expression used for the sake of teaching the masses. Kajimura believes that this concept of Buddha is an expedient means used to teach understanding of *shizen*; (1988:180) the true Buddha is shapeless and can be described only as a wonder. This state of wonder is *shizen*. He believes that Zen Buddhism also has a concept similar to

68

shizen. It is concluded that the Japanese understand *kami* and Buddhas as *shizen* (nature) beyond human knowledge, and that they find the right way to live by following the principles of nature with all their strength. (1988:196)

Although Kajimura over-generalizes the way that the founders of the great religions popularised their ideas, his thesis helps us to understand the relationship between the motif of self-surrender and Japanese supernaturalism. Japanese people have a desire to unite themselves with supernatural beings through self-surrender. The characteristics of the Samurai spirit, such as selflessness, fortitude, courage, resourcefulness, sense of camaraderie, and the spirit of self-sacrifice, can be understood as the outer manifestation of an inner cohesion between people and the supernatural.

This aspiration toward transcendence is usually hidden in ordinary life. As stated repeatedly, the Japanese felt need is extremely pragmatic and this-worldly oriented. Even when they face their death, their desire does not seem to be to go to paradise, but to be placed in a beautiful cemetery. (Gorai, 1991:11) However, at the deepest level of Japanese consciousness, there is still the yearning for eternity.

3.7 Summary

The aim of this chapter has been to clarify the relationship between Japanese supernaturalism and other worldview themes such as syncretism, groupism, contextual logic, life cycle, form consciousness, and self-surrender. Each of the themes needs to be treated as part of a structurally integrated worldview because of the complicated inter-relationships between the themes. As observed above, Japanese supernaturalism has deep interactions with these other worldview themes, and functions to support them. Now we turn to examine the major characteristics of Japanese supernaturalism itself.

Chapter 4

Characteristics of Japanese Supernaturalism

In the previous chapter, we saw briefly Hiebert's analytical framework for religious systems (Figure 10 on page 60) and discussed the fact that the upper zone, the world of transcendence, is either missing or largely absent from a traditional Japanese worldview (Figure 12 on page 61) which is strongly middle-zone-oriented. In short, in Hiebert's terminology, Japanese supernaturalism is fully animistic.

In this worldview, power has priority over truth. An animistic worldview is ruled by pragmatism. This anthropocentric pragmatism allows people to seek this-worldly benefit (*genze riyaku*). While "high religions" are concerned ultimately with truth and salvation, for people in an animistic context, power is the central issue. They ask questions about

Level	Focus	Questions
Religion	Truth	Ultimate origins and destiny Meanings and purpose in life
Animism	Power	Well-being: Disease, famine, drought, etc. Guidance: Fear, uncertainty of the future Success: Failure Peace: Dealing with spirit world and possession
Science	Control	Control of nature by technology: hostile world and difficulties Social harmony: social conflict, wars, rivalries, feuds, etc.

Table 5: Focus and Questions of Explanation Systems (Hiebert, 1990:21)

supernaturally-oriented needs in their actual daily life, such as well-being, guidance, success, and peace. (See table 5.)

Supernatural power has two opposite faces in its dealings with human beings. Hirano points out the instability of the ancient Japanese when coping with the *kami*. They understood *kami* to be two-sided: *nigimitama* (*kami* in friendly relations) and *aremitama* (*kami* in fearsome relations). Hirano believes that this two-sidedness relates to the Japanese view of nature.

> They understand *kami* as objects of awe and intimacy. Once hit by a typhoon, nature displays its brutality but when it leaves it restores calmness and peace. This kind of experience of the changes in nature must have led the people to think that

72

> *kami* have two faces: *nigimitama* and *aremitama*.
> (Hirano, 1982:207–208)

Japanese supernaturalism can be analyzed in two categories using two key concepts: "good fortune consciousness" and "bad fortune consciousness." One is related to *nigimitama* and the other is related to *aremitama*. (See Yonemura 1986:107.)

The reason why we have coined the term "good fortune consciousness" is due to the fact that the distributor of grace in Japanese religious thought is conceptualized somewhat fuzzily. Japanese lack the category of a God who blesses, as found in the God of the Judeo-Christian tradition. The source of the life-affirming power that we are calling 'grace' is grasped in vague terms, as a kind of cosmic supporting power or life force. For most people, the power behind the blessing is dim and vague, like something barely visible in a fog.

In contrast, the objects that bring curses upon the Japanese are considered to be relatively perspicuous. People sometimes may have unhappy spirits who bring them a curse. When that happens, it is assumed that an unhappy spirit who is not being adequately cared for is causing hindrances and problems to its kin. Although in many cases the source of the curse cannot be identified, it is clear that people's fear has a close connection with their death.

4.1   Good Fortune Consciousness

What are the objects of worship or trust for Japanese people? As observed above, they are not found in an absolute existence apart from the natural world. *Kami* are anything that can inspire in a person feelings of awe, reverence, or mystery.

Shinto deities are called *kami*, a term at once singular and plural. The *kami* are numerous, even innumerable, as is suggested by the phrase *yaoyorozu no kami* ("vast myriads of kami"). Originally, any form of existence that possessed some extraordinary, awe-inspiring quality was called *kami*. Mountains, seas, rivers, rocks, trees, birds, animals—anything that evoked awe was regarded as *kami*. Human beings who had some extraordinary quality, people like emperors, heroes, *uji*, or family ancestors, etc., were also referred to as *kami*. It will be evident, therefore, that the *kami* idea held by most Japanese people is essentially different from the idea of God found in the Judeo-Christian and Muslim traditions. (Japan Ministry of Culture, 1972:14)

The survival of this view of deities is clarified when one examines the introduction of Buddhism. As Watanabe (1978), Yamaori (1983) and many others point out, the process of Buddhist indigenization was at the same time a process of transformation.

In the minds of the Japanese rulers, the Buddha was seen as a super-*kami*, the source of a magical power even greater that that of the Shinto *kami*, to be used to ensure political tranquillity, health and prosperity, protection in battle, and protection from natural calamities. (Cook, 1975:219)

Ishida (1983) examines the origin of the Shinto concept of *kami* and finds it in the primitive ages. It is seen as the mystical power of life or the power of production. People are believed to renew and increase the power through worship in integrated community festivals.

Examining the teaching of the new religions, Tsushima et al. (1986) call the common structure of their teaching "a life-oriented view of salvation." They assume that the idea at the core of the teachings, an idea which indeed functions as their entire teaching, is the concept of original life. According to the new religions, there is a kind of Trinity comprised of the cosmos, the gods, and life itself. The whole cosmos is an integrated living being, and everything that exists as a part of the cosmos is essentially connected together by the bond of life. The trust these religions hold in the rejuvenating energy and vital growth energy of life as seen in nature leads them to an attitude of unique optimism. Human beings are given eternal grace by their source of life, like children cared for and nurtured by their mother. They are saved by recovering harmony with the source of life of the cosmos. New religions, which emerged after the 19th century among the Japanese masses, have superseded the traditional religiosity which is characterized by the worship of the life-affirming power.

There are some scholars who feel the primal Shinto ideas were formed during the Jomon or hunter-gatherer period.[1] Umehara calls the Jomon culture "the civilization of the forest" and insists:

> In order to overcome the present-day crises of human civilization, we must return to the wisdom of the starting point—the original idea

[1] A neolithic cultural period extending from about 8,000 B.C. or earlier to about 200 B.C.

of the "other world"—which regards all living beings as basically equal and regards life as a continuous eternal cycle of life and death. (Umehara, 1990:23)

Saji (1990:233) presents the universal character of *Amaterasu* (the sun goddess of Shinto) as a great goddess of love and peace who supplies light and water to every living being and keeps the green Earth from the expanding desert. He contends that the belief in *Amaterasu*, the spirit of the Earth, supported nature worship and a primitive democracy in the Jomon era. These two scholars indicate that re-evaluation of the ancient animistic worldview, which emphasizes harmony between people and nature, would contribute to solving current ecological problems.

In the Yayoi period,[2] the same belief in the life-giving power was succeeded by the agricultural religion, which brought with it some transformations. The spirits of rice were believed to be a source of life-power and they became identified with human spirits. The fertility of the rice spirits leads to increase in the energy level of the human spirit. The common custom of eating rice balls is practiced even today on the occasion of seasonal festivals, in order to regenerate the human spirit through the symbol of the spirit of the rice. The round figure of the rice ball has been shaped after the form of the human heart. (Iwai, 1986:136)

It can be said that the Japanese people were impressed by the luxuriant life-power of the forest in the Jomon period and the abundant productive-power of rice in the Yayoi period.

---

[2] From 200 B.C. to A.D. 200; rice cultivation was introduced at this period

This led them to seek to attain harmony with the creative power in nature and seek to become one with it.

Swyngedouw (1985 in Ogata 1987) points out that in a Japanese traditional community, religions were united by a belief that celebrated production power. Even though local communities are currently breaking down, this belief still remains in the business community, whose aim is to promote production. Therefore, religious rites are often practiced and this is believed to reinforce faith in the company. Reid (1991:39) points to the Toyokawa Inari (a famous shrine dedicated to the fox deity) as symbolic of the shifting continuities of Japanese religion. Inari, the fox deity, was once venerated as a god of the rice harvest, but now is equally popular as a god of business.

Mita (1965:154) asserts that the Japanese religion is a humanistic religion that is not concerned with a transcendent God. The Japanese do not have the category "God" in the Hebrew-Christian sense. In Japan the gods are evaluated by human criteria such as the extent to which they contribute to the happiness of humankind; their religion is wonder-working and divine benefit-oriented.

In the world of monotheism, it is the existence of God that gives ultimate meaning and value to everything. Nature and humanity, then, derive meaning and value from God but have been damaged by sin. Pantheism, however, insists that human life and nature are valuable in and of themselves and sin is understood as a partial, contemporary, surface stain. Human life itself is valued without any relationship to a transcendent God. Pantheists do not think that they need a transcendent God to impart meaning to life. The Japanese have a "consciousness of original grace" in Mita's terminology, while the Westerner's fundamental ethical consciousness is based on the teaching of "original sin". The Japanese have an innate sense for finding beauty or brightness in everything that exists.

Mita explains good fortune consciousness through many illustrations, such as common Japanese customs of keeping a diary, taking snapshots, and the *haiku*[3] form. One of his illustrations is the use of idiomatic phrases such as *itadakimasu* (literally meaning "I take this meal") and *gochisosama* (literally meaning "Thank you for the good meal"), which Japanese use at the beginning and end of meals. Mita points out that these expressions have no specific object to which they are addressed; that is, Japanese are grateful when they can live without trouble in the flow of their lifes, and for this reason they use such expressions.

People seek to harmonize themselves with their outside world and empathize with it. The cosmos itself is familiar to them and at the same time absolute. They do not accept the existence of any absolute apart from their tangible world, and they do not need to seek eternal peace or purely absolute values, or to be liberated from chaotic, troublesome phenomena. This is the reason why this-worldly benefits attract people into Japanese religious communities. The Japanese have an ability to recognize the sacredness of the creature, while of course they have no idea of the Biblical account of creation.

Good fortune consciousness is associated with their grace-giving land surrounded by the sea. They identify themselves with the soft circulation of climatic seasonal changes. It is natural for them to keep an intimate relationship with nature.

[3] A traditional seventeen-syllabled poem.

They enjoy the worldly life and thank the cosmos of which they feel they are a part.

It is not difficult to anticipate the worship of life-giving, cosmos-supporting power—whether the name is *Amaterasu* or *Inari* or *Kannon*—from within the context of good fortune consciousness. *Kami* represents a life force, a source and manifestation of energy found in the world. People, as benefactors of the benefits of that force, are expected to be the upholders of life and its goodness.

However, the nature of *kami* can be seen to be somewhat dualistic. Just as nature itself, they are unpredictable and, as humans, are prone to pique, jealousy, rage and other disturbing habits that can disrupt the flow of life, causing problems, and so the actions and rituals of Japanese supernaturalism largely center on the development and maintenance of good relationships with these life-giving beings.

> [*Kami*] therefore need to be treated correctly: honored, propitiated, venerated and thanked in order to maintain a balanced and productive relationship that can benefit the natural order (and hence human beings living in the world) and to direct their energies into creative rather than destructive directions. (Reader, 1991:27)

Purification rituals are performed to eradicate the pollution of the mundane so as to symbolically bring humans closer to the realms of supernatural beings. People also perform rituals of respect, veneration, propitiation and offering, seeking to gain access to the life-giving powers of spiritual beings.

4.2   Bad Fortune Consciousness

A noticeable inclination of the younger generation is their openness to mysticism. The following diagram (Figure 14 on the facing page) is a summary of a survey conducted by Mainichi Newspaper from November 29 to December 1, 1985. Respondents were randomly chosen.[4]

It is noteworthy that many of those in their twenties have a deep interest in supernatural spiritual powers. We can also see the tendency to support mysticism not only among those in their twenties but also in the children's world: Satan, witchcraft, malevolent deities, phantoms, and diviners have become the characters of animation, software for family computers, plastic models, and cards. (Asahi Newspapers, 1990:40)

Hoshino and Symbol Creation (1991) forecast that the trends of occultism, New Religious Movements and the import of New Age culture will become rooted in the soil of youth culture. They provide three analyses of the background to this tendency:

- **Identity crisis.** Materialistic saturation has brought them to a spiritual hunger and to a lack of orientation and life meaning.

- **Need for community consciousness.** As a result of the identity crisis, a sense of the emptiness of life and ineffectiveness of communication has lead the younger generation to seek a sense of solidarity and a sense of community in the New Religious Movements.

[4]2,321 persons from different parts of Japan. Male 47%, female 53%. 20s 14%, 30s 23%, 40s 23%, 50s 19%, 60s and up 21%.

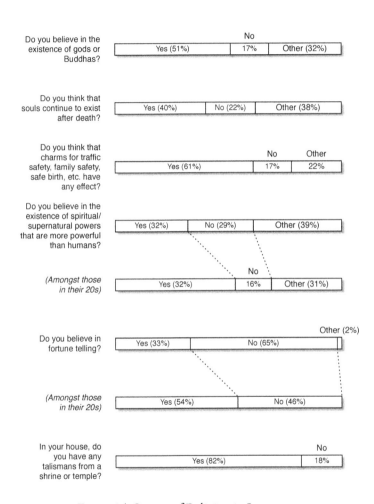

Figure 14: Survey of Religion in Japan

- **Seeking a new value system.** People seek new value systems that overcome decadent problems, such as the ecological crisis, the disintegration of the socialist countries, and the corruption of the capitalist nations.

Nishiyama (1988a:172) claims that all of these things relate to post-Weberian problem consciousness, which asks questions like "how does religion resist modernization?" and "how can religion overcome the negative effects of modernization?" This attention to spiritual powers represents a resistance to the increasing structuralization and rationalization of contemporary society, an emotional counterbalance which is both response and escape. The expansion of "controlled society" brings with it human standardization, uniformity, and conformity, all of which hinder individual self-expression and self-realization and lead to a further erosion of the individual's sense of self-assurance. (Minami, 1987:93)

> For young people caught up in the pressures of the heavily structured Japanese education system with its strong inclinations towards facts and rote learning and its inherent bias against personal expression and analytical discussion, the world of miracles, spirits and mysterious happenings provides a ready means of mental escape, of self-expression and of emotional solace otherwise denied them. (Reader, 1991:236)

Japanese youth are becoming increasingly isolated and individualistic in negative reaction to the "controlled society." One example of this individualistic phenomena is called the "capsule syndrome" (*hikikomori*), which means a sociological inclination where a person shuts him/herself up in a small space, like a capsule. The number of people who are over 30 years old and not married is increasing. Nuclear families are increasingly divorcing and becoming isolated individuals. Moreover, there are many so-called "capsule hotels" in urban areas. These are modern cheap lodgings used by businessmen who cannot return to their home due to their midnight business or drinking associations after business. Their rooms are surprisingly small, like a capsule, which is just larger than the human body. Recently a device was designed to help businessmen relax called a "floatation capsule". It is a small tank half-filled with liquid. A person lies in the tank and experiences a state of weightlessness in order to release him/herself from daily stress.

> The capsule syndrome will continue to advance in the future, and this tendency for people to seek lonely sensual pleasure in an isolated small, secret chamber will become stronger. In this present-day society where there is a lot of stress, the capsule syndrome is manifested in various situations. However at the same time, the background situation to the capsule syndrome should be considered. It is the case that people who seek isolation in the capsule suddenly try to belong to a group organization, which is usually a religious group. The fact that many young people participate in old or new religions is deeply related to this capsule syndrome. (Asahi Newspapers, 1990:22)

Nowadays Japanese have a need for reassurance in their identities. Many urban inhabitants, uprooted from traditional

83

society where they could confirm their identity, are seeking a sense of peace of mind and a sense of feeling at ease and at home, which is lacking in modern life. Many urban youth gradually have lost their ability to maintain their relationships with others due to this on-going process of individualization. This phenomenon is called "contact-fear syndrome." They are having an identity crisis.

Why do they seek the answer to this crisis in the spiritual realms? The bad fortune consciousness, another key concept of Japanese supernaturalism, provides the explanation. Japanese have a fundamental fear that malevolent spirits–particularly those who died angrily–might damage the living. It has been common since the earliest times to interpret the misfortune of physical, mental, or spiritual crisis as being caused by unhappy spirits. Angry, unsettled spirits of the deceased have been believed to hinder the fortunes, health, and happiness of the living, especially those of their family lineage.

Hirano (1982:199–200) contemplates the phrase *chihayaburu*, a conventional epithet for *kami* used in the Man'yoshu[5], interpreting *chihayaburu kami* to mean "gods who act with strong, dangerous power." He thinks that this idea is a major element of the old layer of the Japanese view of the gods. (See Nishiyama 1988b:215.) As Matsugi (1991:36) points out, the ancient people held a severe fear of death. Decomposing bodies and epidemics which occurred caused by the bodies were the core of their fear. It is natural that this fear of death would easily be connected to a fear of dead spirits.

This bad fortune consciousness still remains strong in contemporary Japan. As stated above, communities and families where once ancestor veneration was performed have

---

[5] A famous ancient book of poems.

now disintegrated, so bad fortune consciousness may emerge as an explanation system for the spiritual cause of any crisis. Many new religions teach that problems develop when one fails to take heed of the spiritual repercussions of one's actions. An unhappy spirit who is not cared for causes hindrances and problems to its kin until some recognition of its plight is made and the necessary rituals are performed to pacify it.

It is extremely common for those who are in *yakudoshi*, the unlucky year,[6] to go to a shrine or temple to purchase amulets for protection and receive special purification rites (*harai*) to symbolically sweep away the potential misfortunes and dangers believed to surround people during this year. *Mizuko kuyo*, memorial rites for the souls of aborted fetuses, is one of the most prominent phenomena of recent decades throughout the Japanese religious world. They are performed both by new religions and at many Buddhist temples.

Counter-rituals with strongly purificatory and exorcistic themes have been performed against the unhappy spirits, largely at Buddhist temples. Their powers have long been invoked not just to transform the dead soul into an ancestor but also to hem in and restrict the dangerous, polluting and angry repercussions of death. The new religions, too, provide the means, via rituals and spiritual healing techniques, through which such hindrances may be removed and through which unhappy spirits may be soothed. The spiritual malevolence of the distressed ancestral spirits is purified by this means.

Yoshino (1983) discusses the great influence of Yin-yang magic in the spiritual history of Japan. Takemitsu (1991) acknowledges that the shamanistic manipulation of spiritual power has taken various styles in Japanese history: *araburu*

---

[6]33 for a woman and 42 for a man.

kami, (wild *kami*), *tokoyo no kami* (*kami* in other world), developed Yin-yang magic, esoteric Buddhism and the like. He, however, asserts that this shamanistic stream should be called "Japanese philosophy," which the ancient people attained from the observation of nature. Japanese people have tried to overcome the bad fortune consciousness by Japanese supernaturalism.

> Japanese festivals and folk customs have not just merely consisted of venerating *kami* as "our precious *kami*," but sometimes have been in conflict with *kami* to make a stand against damage caused by wind and water. (Yoshino, 1983:236)

Contemporary Japanese also tend to manipulate spiritual power through religious means to get an answer for their identity crisis, their isolation and an expected new paradigm that can overcome the decadent problems.

4.3   Summary

Japanese supernaturalism can be analyzed in terms of two concepts: good fortune consciousness and bad fortune consciousness. The Japanese have a good fortune consciousness, which leads people to seek to harmonize themselves with their outside world and empathize with it. They enjoy their worldly life and give thanks to the cosmos, which they themselves are a part of. In the context of this good fortune consciousness it is natural for them to worship a life force, a source and manifestation of energy. So the actions and rituals of Japanese supernaturalism largely center on the development and maintenance of harmonious relationships with life-giving spiritual beings.

Another key concept of Japanese supernaturalism is bad fortune consciousness, which provides the explanation of their crises. Japanese have a fundamental fear that malevolent spirits might damage the living. It is believed that an unhappy spirit who was not cared for causes hindrances and problems to its kin until some amount of recognition of its plight has been made and the necessary rituals are performed to pacify it. Counter-rituals with strong purificatory and exorcistic themes are performed against the unhappy spirits, so that the hindrances may be removed and unhappy spirits may be soothed.

People maintain supernaturalism for treating the gods correctly: honoring and thanking them in order to maintain a balanced and productive relationship and to direct their energies in creative rather than destructive directions. And people perform counter-rituals with strongly purificatory and exorcistic themes against the unhappy spirits in order to remove spiritual blockage or hindrances and sources of psychic retribution or pollution.

Chapter 5

Rituals of Japanese Religion

Since worldview is the generator and integrator of the total cultural system, it is what generates various subsystems. Japanese supernaturalism is systematically interrelated with the Japanese religious subsystem. The aim of this chapter is to examine the religious rituals and the relationship between these rituals with Japanese supernaturalism.

As explained in section 2.3.3 on page 21, each subsystem consists of at least three of the following characteristics: assumptions, rituals and creative behavior. In this chapter, ritual and creative behavior are the focus, as well as how the Japanese worldview affects the structure of the rituals. The assumptions of the religious subsystems have been treated in the previous chapters as part of the explanation of the worldview assumptions, so I will not include a section on this here.

5.1 Functions of Ritual

Japanese religious rituals are intended to ward off or decrease any misfortune and secure or augment the cooperation of the *kami* in promoting the happiness and peace of the individual and the community. The focus of the rituals of Japanese religion is to harmonize people with *kami*, to gain access to their life-giving powers through maintaining a balanced and productive relationship with these *kami*.

Mayumi presents a useful perspective as a contemporary Shintoist. He defines the Shinto shrine as the sacred world separated from the secular world, where people regain their divinity and the reinforcement of social solidarity.

> The change in quality from living in the secular world to living in the sacred world, which is expressed in Japanese terms as "from *ke* to *hare*", makes people regain their divinity and reconfirms the meaning of social life. To regain their divinity generally means "*o-kage o itadaku*" (obtain the grace of *kami*) or "*goriyaku o koumuru*" (receive benefit). In other words, it means to live a productive life in hope and power by revering the authority of the *kami*, believing in the *kami*'s grace and living joyfully in the protection of *kami*. (Mayumi, 1984:17)

The motifs of unity with divinity and of the divine community can be found in this understanding. The divine-human unification as well as the human-human unification takes place within the holy shrine. And due to its holiness, its separateness from the secular, people expect hope and power from *kami*. *Kami* are seen as gracious and authoritative. It can be said that Japanese try to manipulate the *kami's* power through rituals which are designed to attain human unification in and with *kami*.

The community aspect cannot be ignored, especially in contemporary urban settings. Many New Religious Movements provide their followers with a nexus of identity and self-confidence on individual and social levels. In this age of disintegration of the local communities, they represent the spiritual homeland (*kokoro no furusato*) of the Japanese people that is lacking in modern life. (See Reader 1991:239–241.)

A survey conducted around 1970 of people who visited shrines showed that sixty-six percent of the men and seventy-five percent of the women interviewed experienced what they called *aratamatta kimochi*, a feeling of inner renewal. (Picken, 1980:56) The major function of Shinto rituals is to reaffirm the sense of renewal and sense of community.

In crisis situations, people expect other functions from the rituals. The belief in the disruptive influence of unnatural and premature death and its resultant pollution has lead Japanese to introduce counter-rituals against the unhappy spirits. The counter rituals usually take the form of purification rituals (*harai*). They are performed to eradicate the impediments of the mundane, so as to symbolically bring humans closer to the realms of the *kami*.

The root cause of physical events is assumed to be located in the spiritual realm. The first task, then, is to identify the spiritual blockage or hindrance (*sawari*, *reisho*), any source of psychic retribution (*tatari*) or the nature of the pollution (*kegare*) which may be impeding the productive powers of life.

The cause of the problems are often sought in ritual neglect, which is believed to allow pollution and hindrances to develop. (For example, the failure to carry out the proper memorial services.)

Therefore the process of removal of the pollution and hindrances involves ritual action with strongly purificatory and exorcistic themes. Such motifs are central to Buddhist rituals for the dead; *harai*, Shinto purification rituals; *o-kiyome*, a technique of spiritual healing in Mahikari;[1] and *hoshimatsuri*, the Buddhist fire rituals of Agonshu.[2] Through these rituals, such hindrances are believed to be removed and unhappy spirits are presumed to be soothed or transformed into kind guardians. This transformation of the malevolent spirits into benevolent ones is accompanied with a motif of renewal and revitalization.

Picken points out that the *yakubarai* (purification rites) is sometimes, but incorrectly, translated as "exorcism."

> In the West, exorcism implies removing a devil. In Shinto, *yakubarai* means merely the calming of a troublesome *kami* who has been offended by some impurity. (Picken, 1980:53)

The tendency of the Japanese to avoid confrontation even against the destructive *kami* can be observed here. *Harai* is intended to remove the polluting power, but it is performed in a harmonious way.

[1] One of the New Religious Movements.
[2] Another New Religious Movement.

5.2 Types of Rituals

The Shinto and Buddhist practices of ordinary people may be grouped under two headings: the annual cycle and the life cycle. The rituals are analyzed under these headings, with a third category added for crisis rites.

5.2.1 Annual Festivals

Many types of annual festivals are observed which have a relationship with the seasonal rice producing process and ancestor veneration traditions. (See Figure 15 on the following page.)

New Year Shrine/Temple Visit (*hatsumode*) The most important festival of the annual cycle rites are the New Year rites and the Bon festival. (midsummer festival of lights). According to police estimates, 80 million (nearly 65% of the population) visited a big-name shrine or temple at the beginning of the new year in 1990. The purpose of this practice was to receive new spiritual power from *kami* through worship and purification rites.

Bon Festival The Bon Festival is a community activity in which, traditionally, individual households welcome their visiting ancestral spirits and entertain them communally. Even today, millions of people travel to the country for the Bon Festival family reunions and return to the cities a few days later. Today, the Bon Festival is highly secularized and regarded as merely family reunion or vacation especially by urban nuclear

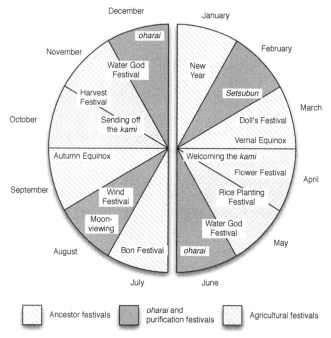

Note that the above dates are based on the traditional lunar calendar.

Figure 15: Pattern of Major Annual Festivals (Reid, 1991:24)

families. Some New Religious Movements teach that ritual observance by the living kin provides them with a connection with the welfare of their ancestors in the next world, so neglected ancestral spirits may punish the living with ill fortune, sickness or the threat of death if they do not conduct this ritual.

5.2.2 Life Cycle Rites

The life cycle rites mark transitions between different statuses and roles and changes in membership. (See Figure 13 on page 63.) They focus on individual rites, but their context is the family.

Pre-birth rites Couples who are waiting for the birth of their baby visit certain shrines (*ubuzunagami*) which function for this purpose (*kosazuke*). Alternatively, they attend their village shrine (*chinju*) or tutelary shrine (*ujigami*).

Birth rites (*obiiwai* and *anzankigan*) In the fifth month of pregnancy, a woman with child puts on a white stomach band (*iwataobi*). This rite, the *obiiwai*, is the first acknowledgment of the baby's life by the extended family. Often at the same time a prayer for an easy delivery is made (*anzankigan*).

Naming (*nazuke*) The date of naming a baby differs depending on past and local tradition, but a typical celebration (*oshichiya*) is conducted on the seventh day. People name the baby and display the name in the home altar or in the *tokonoma* (alcove), announcing it to the relatives and acquaintances by hosting a party. The naming holds the meaning of acknowledging the baby to the extended family and the local community.

Report to the Shrine (*hatsumiyamairi*) After about 30 days, the shrine is visited again by the couple with the baby, in thanksgiving for protection and for reporting the birth to the *kami*. This ritual is about the acknowledgment of the baby as a human being before the *kami*. If the shrine they choose is a tutelary shrine (*ujigami*), this ritual has an additional meaning in that the baby gets a membership in the traditional worship community (the *uji*).

Shichi-Go-San (**Seven-Five-Three**) *Shichi-Go-San* is the celebration for children who have reached the ages of seven, five and three years. The combination of age and sex differs depending on the locality. Family members attend the shrine to thank the *kami* and ask for protection in the future while dressing their 7-, 5-, and 3-year-old children in their best clothes. On November 15, parents and children go to shrines and visit relatives, and memorial pictures are taken of the children in their best clothes. A type of candy called *chitose-ame* is sold on this occasion because sweet candies used to be considered a substitute for the mothers' milk. Until age seven, children's lives are considered to be included within the life of the *kami* as life-giving power (*shichisai madewa kami no uchi*), and from then on, they are regarded as having an independent personality.

University Entrance This is not a traditional rite, but has a tremendous impact on Japanese youth today. All children in Japan face what is usually called "examination hell," the fiery ordeal of competition for places in top-ranking universities, graduation from which will virtually guarantee a secure job and social status. Life for the Japanese child is a series of examination hurdles, all of which are important. Students and their families go to *tenjin* shrines where the *kami* of learning is enshrined, and offer *ema* (wooden prayer-tablets that are hung on trees at shrines or found in small buildings specially erected to house them) for success in their examinations.

Adult Day Celebration (*seijin no hi*) A national holiday, held on January 15 each year, marks the formal coming-of-age celebrations of the nation's twenty-year-olds. On this day these young adults are invited to their local town halls to attend lectures and other events. Then, formally dressed (women in *furisode* or long-sleeved kimonos), they make their way in thanksgiving to a nearby shrine. From this day on, they are regarded as responsible members of society and enfranchised with all the rights of citizenship, including voting rights. Many elements of old initiation rites remain in this celebration. In former days, boys around fifteen and girls around thirteen were regarded as adults after various rituals and permitted to join the association of young adults (*wakamono-gumi* for male or *musume-gumi* for female). "Adult Day is one example of how Shinto has been absorbed into modern institutions, helping to integrate them into a fuller view of the flow of life." (Picken, 1980:28)

Marriage Although these days it is not unusual for a wedding to be held in a Christian church, around 80% of ceremonies still take place in Shinto shrines. Before the Meiji era (1868–1912), marriage ceremonies were not held in shrines but in family houses. In principle, marriage was a matter for the couples' families and not for the couples themselves because it meant the transfer of labor. Nowadays, this intent survives, but marriage and the marriage service is becoming more individualistic.

The ritual of marriage consists of three ceremonies: 1) *yuino*, confirmation of the engagement; 2) *kekkonshiki*, wedding ceremony and 3) *hiro'en*, reception. Both families report the couple's marriage to the *kami*, pray for freedom from ill fortune and pray for the blessing of good things. Purification rites (*harai*) and a sharing of a holy feast (*sansankudo*) with the *kami* invoked also take place at the ceremony, which marks the transition of social status from unmarried to married and unites the households through matrimony.

Funerals (*soshiki*) Generally, funerals are conducted according to Buddhist rites. Their emphasis is on the divine-human continuum and so the function of the funerals can be summarized in three points: 1) to send the deceased to the other world (a triumphal return to the source of life; see Fujii 1985:152); 2) to purify the family and the house from the pollution of death; and 3) to provide an occasion to pay respect to the deceased. (A concrete expression of thanksgiving to the deceased spirits; see Hanayama 1991:11.)

Ancestor Veneration (*houji*) The process of becoming an ancestor calls for 33 to 50 years of ritual observances, some

98

at the Buddhist temple, others before the Buddhist altar in the home. The 49th day, 100th day, one year, and three years after the death are believed to be especially important. Conflicting emotions—fear of the deceased spirit and condolences to the dead family member—are the central motifs of *houji*.

5.2.3 Rites of Crisis

Crisis rites are rituals used to prevent or deal with crises such as illness, drought, fire, earthquakes, failure in love, evil spirits, curses, pollution and/or the destructive *kami*.

Calming the spirit of an offended kami (*Yakubarai*)   There are several kinds of *kami* who bring disaster, (*yakujin*) such as *yakubyogami* (*kami* of plague), *binbogami* (*kami* of poverty), and *shinigami* (*kami* of death). These need to be calmed because they are rulers of disaster. Through the influence of Taoism came a belief that when people reach certain ages (*yakudoshi*) they should be discreet and careful in their behavior because their ages are cursed. This belief has spread widely and is believed by many people today. In general, the ages that are recognized as the disastrous years (*yakudoshi*) are 10, 25, 42 and 61 for men, and 19, 33 and 37 for women. The age of 42 for men and 33 for women is called *taiyaku* (the great disastrous age), so those who reach that age are thought to be in danger not only at that age, but also the days before and after (*maeyaku/atoyaku*). There are several ways to avoid disasters, yet the typical way is to visit a shrine (*yakujin*) and ask the *kami* to remove the curses (*tatari*) through the purification rites in which the priest performs *yakubarai* to calm the *kami*. *Yakubarai* has an invisible, magical power to transform human beings. (Mitsuhashi, 1984:7) Surprisingly, this belief has permeated to the grass roots level of the Japanese mentality.

Ground-breaking ceremony (*jichinsai*)   The ceremony of *jichinsai* is conducted to purify the site of a new building. It is intended to seek the cooperation and protection of the *kami*. When the basic framework of the building is completed, and the first vertical beam is raised to roof level, there is *muneage-shiki*, the ceremony of raising the framework. When the building is completed, openings are marked by a Shinto ceremony (*shunko-shiki*). Purification rites related to the building construction are applied to public buildings as well as to hotels and large projects in civil engineering. Moreover, purification rites are widely practiced in every phase of Japanese life such as at the inauguration service of nuclear power stations or ultra-modern computer factories. These rituals are used to prevent crises caused by *kami* of disaster.

Omamori (amulets) and *ofuda* (charms)   According to the survey cited above (Mainichi Newspaper, 1986), half of the Japanese people have amulets which are used for traffic safety, recovery from illness, protection from evil, success in university entrance examinations and prospects for marriage. This tendency is strong in the younger generation and 58% of those in their 20s answered positive to the same question. Even a space rocket launcher is plastered with amulets. (Mayumi, 1984:229) The same survey reports that 82% of the

Japanese have charms in their homes. The role of the amulets and charms used by the Japanese to provide a sense of safety is far more spiritual than one might expect. Most Japanese think that tablets empowered by Shinto shrines or Buddhist temples do contain some kind of spiritual power.

Healing (*byoki heiyu*) The Shinto shrine has also functioned as a place of prayer for the sick. There are many special shrines that are famous for the results of healing prayer. Most New Religious Movements emphasize healing, and this approach is extremely successful today because of the increasing health consciousness and the openness to spiritual activity.

5.3 Structure of Ritual (*Ketsuke* Ritual)

This perspective on the supernatural activities of *kami*, whose main function is giving life power, provides a useful explanation of the ideology of *matsuri* (festivals) and rituals. Sakurai (1985), Sonoda (1977), and Miyata (1983) develop the theory of *kegare*, a controversial ethnological term. In this situation, life energy, or *ke*, is interpreted as running quite low, like a dried-up lake. In order to preserve their daily routines, people need *ke* as a source of energy or vitality. *Ke* radiates its energy to retain the ordinary situation and gradually declines in energy and weakens functionally. That is to say that ordinary life shifts to *kegare*. People need to perform a ritual to revitalize and reinforce the vitality of *ke* to avoid functional disorder and the diminishing of productive activity. This ritual of revitalization and reinforcement is called *hare*. This circulation from *ke* to *kegare*, *kegare* to *hare*, *hare* to *ke* continues to be held so that

101

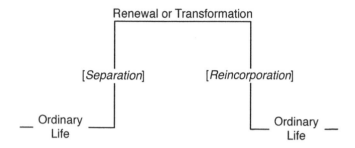

Figure 16: Stages of Rituals (Hiebert, 1990:116)

normal human life, normal functions of human society and the survival of the community would be preserved. Nishiyama (1988b:207) calls this ritual *ketsuke*.

The *ketsuke* ritual can be diagramed using the three stage model described Hiebert (1990) and others.[3] (See figure 16.) Hiebert's model has been modified for the *ketsuke* ritual, and the energy factor has been added to the diagram. (Figure 17 on the next page.)

Rituals are characterized by three stages, 1) separation, in which people "separate" themselves from normative behaviors of the daily world, 2) transformation, the actual change taking place by engaging in the ritual, and 3) reincorporation, a reintroduction into society of the ritualized people.

The stages of the *ketsuke* ritual can be superimposed on the above ritual pattern to demonstrate the depletion and reinvigoration of *ke*. In the separation stage, the abundance of *ke* dries up, leading to the state of *kegare*; it then becomes

---

[3]For instance, Van Gennep, Leach, and Turner.

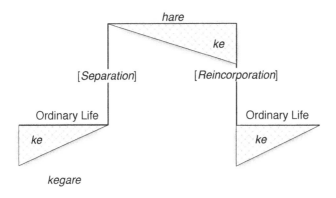

Figure 17: Stages of the *Ketsuke* Ritual

replenished as the transformation proceeds, exhausting itself again in the final stage.

Nishiyama correctly points out that, separate to the *ketsuke* function, today's youth are seeking a *tsukitsuke* function which leads them into the realms of luck and magic. *Tsukitsuke* lacks the energy (*ke*) dimension of the *ketsuke* ritual. This distinction can represent a significant breakthrough for the younger generation who often feel bottled-up because their honest labors are not rewarded. (Nishiyama, 1988a:208) The focus on magic for the young people is not a result of their expressive separation from ordinary life, but an actual breaking through the horizon of ordinary life. However, it can be also said that the *tsukitsuke* ritual is an expression of Japanese supernaturalism, where people seek good fortune from within the supernatural realm.

5.4 Conclusion

In the conclusion of part II, we present four questions emerging from the Japanese worldview. They are answered to some extent by the Japanese religions, especially in their ritualistic dimensions.

The first question is associated with the good fortune consciousness of Japanese supernaturalism; that is, "Who gives us life-giving power?" Japanese people know the mystical power of life, or the power of production, that fills the cosmos. They attempt to reinvigorate and expand that power through their worship by means of various religious rituals.

The second question is related to the bad fortune consciousness of Japanese supernaturalism; namely, "Who protects us?" They have a fundamental fear of malevolent spirits and have been seeking a protector from them.

The third question is a reflection of *amae*, the psychological desire to "belong;" it is, "To whom or to what do I belong?" Traditionally, Japanese religious systems have provided an answer to this question. However, people are now facing identity crises because of the disintegration of their local communities. New Religious Movements function somewhat as a "spiritual homeland" for alienated urban youth.

The fourth question is a hidden one. Japanese do aspire to or yearn for that which is transcendental or universal, but this inclination is hidden behind their surface pragmatism. People long for transcendental value by overcoming the conflicts and attachments of ordinary reality and denying the ego-centered self at the deep worldview level. Therefore, the fourth question can be expressed as "How can I reach eternity?"

Part III

Toward an Ethno-Ecclesiology

Chapter 6

Pauline Ecclesiology

Those who intend to develop a contextualized model of church need to examine the biblical data concerning the New Testament church. Specifically, Paul's idea of the Church in his epistles provides rich information, on the basis of which both a Biblically sound and culturally appropriate church model can be constructed. The purpose of this chapter is to investigate the outline of Pauline ecclesiology and to extract from this some missiological implications for Christian communication in Japan.

First, we view the nature of the Church as the people of God from a redemptive-historical perspective, and as the body of Christ from a Christological perspective. Following that, we will examine the practice and organization of the Church based around the key term of "upbuilding."

6.1 The Church as the People of God

Paul sees the Church from two points of view. (Ridderbos, 1975:327) The first is the redemptive-historical perspective, whereby the Church is considered to be the continuation and fulfillment of the historical people of God; the people who, in Abraham, God chose for Himself, and to which He bound Himself in making the covenant and the promises. The second is the Christological perspective, whereby he gives his own form of expression to the existence and character of the church when he speaks of it as the body of Christ.

Both ways of viewing the church are connected, but we will discuss them independently, beginning with the redemptive-historical perspective.

6.1.1 Images of ἐκκλησία and ἅγιοι

There are several metaphors Paul uses to express the redemptive-historical aspects of the church. The word ἐκκλησία needs to be examined first because it occurs about sixty times in his letters.

Εκκλησία has a double history, one being Jewish, the other being Greek. This most prevalent name is used consciously in connection with the Old Testament people of God. The word ἐκκλησία occurs about 100 times in the LXX. The Hebrew equivalent is almost always   . Pauline use of ἐκκλησία is derived from the title of the Old Testament people of God as the   . The frequent use by Paul of the qualification "church of God" is equivalent of   in Deuteronomy. In using this term, Paul indicates who the true people of God are; that is, the Messianic congregation of the great end time.

Banks (1988:49) draws attention to three aspects of Paul's understanding of ἐκκλησία: 1) a voluntary association, with regular gatherings of a relatively small group of like-minded people; 2) the household unit; 3) the visible manifestation of a universal and eternal commonwealth. He asserts that Paul's understanding of ἐκκλησία embraces all three ideas of community to which people gave their commitment in the ancient world at that time. This all-inclusive concept had a decided advantage over its first century competitors, such as those of the Qumran, Pharisaic and Stoic communities. As such it demonstrates Paul's emphasis on the centrality of meeting for community life, which he expressed as an ongoing heavenly encounter with Christ.

The most frequent description Paul gives of the members of the Church is ἅγιοι, which is translated "saints" almost forty times. The naming of Israel can be traced back to the Old Testament as the holy people of God (Exod. 19:6; Lev. 11:44, 45), also expressed as a substantive: "(the) saints," (cf. Deut. 33:3; Num. 16:3; Ps. 16:3; 34:10; 89:6) also in conjunction with "the people" or the "congregation." The empirical Israel qualified themselves as the true people of God, preserved and delivered by the Lord from godlessness and from eschatological judgment. Paul identified the Christian Church as the true people of God, the eschatological Israel.

Although a distinction from Israel is also seen in Paul's letters (which will be treated in the next section), it is clear that Paul takes over the basic idea of a holy people of Israel set apart from ordinary purposes. This difference does not mean withdrawing from the world, but of living differently within it. Barclay asserts that a saint (the Greek word is ἅγιος) is one who is in Christ Jesus.

109

> The difference which the word *hagios* expresses is that the man who is *hagios* lives his life in the constant presence of Jesus Christ, in the constant awareness of that presence, and in the constant and deliberate attempt to listen to the commands of Christ and to carry them out. His life is lived within the world, and within the affairs of the world, but his whole life is dictated by the standards of Christ, and not by the standards of the world. The word 'saints' really means "Christ's dedicated people." Those who are members of the Church are those who have dedicated their lives to Jesus Christ. (Barclay, 1958:239–240)

"The elect," "beloved," and "called" are descriptions of the Church closely linked with the qualification "the saints." They are taken as a designation of the Church by Paul, and also have to be understood with reference to the historical chosenness, love-relationship, and calling of Israel by the Lord.

Paul's view of the Church is not individualistic. He believes that the salvation given in Christ has special reference to the Church and to the individual believer by virtue of belonging to the Church. For example, when he pictures the Church as the bride of Christ (Eph. 5:22–23), he does not mention the individual believer but treats her as a people. A chaste virgin to one husband, Christ (2 Cor. 11:2), the Church is not assumed to be an individual believer. Paul sees the Church not as a gathering of individual believers, but as a collection of people whom God has placed at his side and through whom he intends to exemplify his grace and redemption.

6.1.2   New Concept of Israel

Paul further defines the Church as the continuation of Israel who is the elect, called, holy people of God, since, on the one hand, the Church springs from and is born out of Israel, and, on the other, the Church takes the place of Israel as the historical people of God.

In Romans 4:16, Paul expands the definition of "seed of Abraham" and renews the concept of Israel, the congregation of God, by insisting that Abraham's descendants are not just those who obey the Law, but also those who believe as Abraham did. Similarly, the circumcision is reinterpreted as that which takes place in the heart by the Spirit, not externally in the flesh, by the written Law (Rom. 2:28,29). In Ephesians 2:11 and similar pronouncements, being a Jew and being circumcised acquires a purely spiritual significance, and the natural and empirical factors are no longer taken into account. In the Pauline epistles, natural descent from Abraham is no longer a determinant for belonging to the people of God.

For Paul, the promise of the New Covenant (Jer. 31:33; Ezek. 11:19, 36:26) is one of the great supports of his spiritual and universal definition of the Church as the people of God and the new Israel. "It is on account of this fulfilment of the prophecy of the New Covenant in the Christian church that all the privileges of the Old Testament people of God in this spiritual sense pass over to the church". (Ridderbos, 1975:336) The Church of the New Covenant is distinguished by the forgiveness of sins and the gift of the Spirit. The privileges of the people of God that were once exclusively those of national Israel are now, without distinction, possessed by those who belong to Christ.

111

Faith in the uniqueness and the gracious character of God revealed in Christ supports Pauline universalism. Since God is one and there is no other God, the God known and worshiped by Israel must be the God of the Gentiles (1 Tim. 2:4–6). Since God is gracious and there is no distinction among all humankind, God saves not only Jews, but also Gentiles (Rom. 3:29-30). Paul thus concentrates on the qualitative content of the words of the prophet Hosea and extends the application of the 'not-my-people' and the 'not-beloved' to the Gentiles: "The people who were not mine, I will call 'My People.' The nation that I did not love, I will call 'My Beloved.' And the very place where they were told, 'You are not my people,' there they will be called the sons of the living God." (Rom. 9:25-26) Paul is able to see the Church of the Gentiles as endowed with all the privileges and blessings of Israel, and to see it occupy the place of unbelieving Israel, upholding the continuation of God's original redemptive intentions with historical Israel. Paul is also able to see that in Christ the whole Church, Jews and gentiles together, has become one body of Christ.

6.2   The Church as the Body of Christ

The most characteristic figure of the Church used by Paul is to see the church as a body (Rom. 12:4–5; 1 Cor. 10:17, 12:27). The qualification "body of Christ" is typically Pauline and it describes the christological mode of existence of the Church as the people of God.

6.2.1   Unity of the Body

Paul emphasizes the organic unity of the Church by applying the name "body of Christ" to the Church. It is highly superficial to suppose that this idea of the body is restricted to the mutual unity and diversity of believers. Rather it is qualified as the body that is "in union with Christ." (Rom. 12:5) "Body of Christ" denotes a special, close relationship and communion that exists between Christ and His Church. Paul presents the unity of the body, combining the vertical relationship between Christ and His Church with the horizontal relationship among believers. He does not intend in the first place to qualify its mutual unity and diversity, but to denote its unity in and with Christ.

Allen's emphasis concerning unity of the Church is noteworthy. He believes that the basis of Paul's unity is found in the simple fact that there is one Head and one body.

> St. Paul began with unity. In his view the unity of the Church was not something to be created, but something which already existed and was to be maintained. Churches were not independent unities: they were extensions of an already existing unity. There could be no such thing as two churches in the same place both holding the Head, yet not in communion one with another. There could be no such thing as two churches in different places both holding the Head, yet not in communion one with another. There could be no such thing as a Christian baptized into Christ Jesus not in communion with all the other members of the body of which

> Christ was the Head. If a member was united to
> the Head he was united to all the other members.
> (Allen, 1962a:128)

Furthermore, Allen analyzes the four practical principles of unity drawn from Paul's relationship to the parent church in Jerusalem. Gilliland (1983:201–202) summarizes Allen's citation as follows:

1. Paul refused to transplant the law and the customs of the church in Judea into the four provinces. He let the church express its own life wherever it was.

2. Paul refused to set up any central administrative authority from which the whole church was to receive directions. Rather, each church was entrusted with the responsibility for its own life.

3. Paul declined to establish *a priori* tests of orthodoxy. Laws were not prescribed. It was not stated precisely what a church must think or do in every case.

4. Paul refused to allow the universal application of precedents. What was right for one place may not be appropriate for another. Much less could uniformity of thought or action for all be demanded.

Paul insists that each church must affirm its diversity among churches and respect each other, because all churches belong to each other with interdependent relationships in the body of Christ. The justification for qualifying the Church as the body of Christ lies in the fact that the people of God have unity and common existence in Christ.

6.2.2   Headship of Christ

A noticeable development of Paul's use of the body metaphor can be found in his epistles to the Ephesians and the Colossians. In Romans 12 and 1 Corinthians 12, the Church as the body of Christ is described as a genuine body in unity and diversity. But in Paul's later writings, more markedly than his earlier writings, a spiritual connection emerges between the Church and the glorified Christ.

In the later correspondence, the concept of "head" has its own independent significance and must be understood from the structures and connections of the human community. Headship points to a position of rulership and authority. The spiritual aspect of the body of Christ emerges very clearly in Ephesians and Colossians along with the redemptive-historical aspect. Christ's position of authority as the exalted Lord receives particular emphasis. It is the position of superiority and rulership of the head.

Christ, however, is also the Preserver or Saviour of the body, hence the relationship between the head and body cannot merely be understood as that of the Church subject to Christ. The Church has its origin in Christ. Therefore, it is dependent upon Him to whom it owes its existence. "Head" thus points not merely to superiority, control, rule, but to the beginning. "As the Head Christ so much desires to unite himself by his Spirit with the church and to dwell in it, because it is from him and is one in him and with him." (Ridderbos, 1975:382)

> While in Romans and in 1 Corinthians all
> attention is concentrated on the relation of the
> church as one body, in Colossians and Ephesians
> the bond between Christ and his own itself
> comes into view, especially in its continuing
> pneumatic and all-embracing significance. (Rid-
> derbos, 1975:387)

6.3 The Church as πλήρωμα

In the epistles to the Ephesians and the Colossians, Christ is expressed not only as the Head of his Church but also as the Head of all things that are in heaven and on Earth. What is the connection that Paul makes between Christ's all-embracing significance as the Head of all things, (Eph. 1:22) and his position as the Head of the Church?

God has conferred on Christ superiority above all rule, authority, power and dominion (Eph. 1:21; cf. Col. 1:16, 2:10); on the basis of which, the Bible talks about angelic powers which are subjection to God and those which are in rebellion against God. In Christ's exaltation, his ownership of all things, which he held already at the creation of the world, has taken effect anew (Eph. 1:9, 10). All this has its deepest significance in the fact that all His fullness was pleased to dwell in Christ (Col. 1:19, 2:9). Christ is the Head of all things and of all principalities and powers (Col. 2:10), and, by virtue of this glory, he fills all things (Eph. 4:10, 1:23).

With this concept of fullness, Paul is pitting himself against a religiosity that has been highly conditioned by belief in cosmic powers under which people find themselves in a slavish position of subjection. The thought behind 'Fullness' or 'the Filled One' is that of being outside or above God, over Whom nothing or no one has existence or power. Here Paul presents a message to reach his listeners by entering their frame of reference. He pronounces Christ as One who fills the universe in such a way that the entirety of it falls within reach of his mighty presence. Thus, he focuses on spiritual warfare where the all-embracing and all-transcending power and grace of Christ confronts the principalities, the powers, the world rulers of this darkness and the evil spirits in the heavenly places (Eph. 6:12).

The Church as a domain filled with Christ is distinguished from the universe Christ fills with his mighty presence. The Church refers primarily to the appropriation of the resultant benefits and gifts of Christ to and by the Church, while the universe speaks especially of his power and of the completeness of all things in him. The Church is Christ's πλήρωα (fullness), which is understood as a mandate and a goal, as well as a gift. The fullness of Christ leads the church to draw from Him all that is necessary for its perfecting and growth. The church has received from God an armor against the cosmic powers (Eph. 6:13ff.), so that it may represent and exhibit the fullness of Christ in the world.

6.4 The Upbuilding of the Church

In previous two sections, the nature of the New Testament Church was treated from both the redemptive-historical perspective and the christological perspective. Now we turn to the practice and organization of the Church.

There are two presuppositions with regards to the up-building of the Church. One is that the Church does not immediately reach its final goal. As Gilliland asserts, there is no reason to believe that every sin will quickly cease, or that the members are going to be anything but flesh-and-blood people. (Gilliland, 1983:193) Because the Church consists of real people, it is not perfect. But, because these are people of God for whom Christ died, it is loved by—and will one day be perfectly ruled by—Christ. The Church is in a process of maturation, being moved by a transforming spiritual power, reaching on to the very height of Christ's full stature (Eph. 4:13).

Another presupposition about the upbuilding of the Church, related to the first, is that, in the Church's process of maturation, there is an abiding object of God's care evidenced by progress, extension and consolidation. Paul believes that God wants the church to grow (Col. 2:19) and the growth is the work of God (1 Cor. 3:6). The church is expected to grow up in every way unto Christ in maturation, as well as by numerical increase (Eph. 4:15).

6.4.1   A Family in the House

Paul's "family" terminology is often overlooked because of its rare usage. However, related expressions are so frequent that "family" must be regarded as the most significant metaphorical usage of all. The relationship that exists between Christ, the Christian, and God is basic to this concept. Christians are recognized as members of a divine family, adopted as sons of God (1 Thess. 1:10; Gal. 4:4–5), given the Spirit of his Son in their hearts, so that along with Jesus, they are able to address God in the most intimate terms as "Abba! Father!" (Gal. 4:5-6). This fellowship of Christians with God the Father

118

and Jesus his Son is a most intimate expression of personal interrelationship between God and humankind.

True fellowship as a family produces fruit from within the context of its own life, because believers are free from "sin," the Mosaic law—an instinctive or external moral code—as well as from supernatural agencies and death. As a fundamental freedom, this provides for them a reconciled relationship with God and others, and brings them the life-power of the community as the result of the recovered relationship. Banks writes,

> So this freedom granted by God not only trans-
> fers men and women out of a broken relationship
> with God, and a defective solidarity with men,
> into a new community with both, but also
> inclines them to live the kind of life that will
> extend and deepen that new community itself.
> (Banks, 1988:27)

This community life conveys the freshest, most dynamic appeal to the people. The conversion occurs not merely by words but by an experience of Christ through the supernatural work of the Spirit. Allen popularized the term "spontaneous expansion," describing it as unexhorted and unorganized activities of individual members of the Church explaining to others the Gospel. Allen defines spontaneous expansion as

> the expansion which follows the irresistible
> attraction of the Christian church for men who
> see its ordered life and are drawn to it by
> desire to discover the secret of a life which they
> instinctively desire to share. (Allen, 1962b:7)

119

Fellowship is as a family of witnesses interacting. Spontaneous witness is the response of a healthy organism to the law of its life. It is not the Pauline idea of the Church that it must be first a house wherein people are welcomed and led to Christ. Rather, Paul's confidence is that a new fellowship is, by nature, a witnessing fellowship. In fact, the two expressions–the inner coherence of the body of Christ, and the consolidation of the house of God–are closely connected. It is said of the house of God that it grows up, as a living organism (Eph. 2:21), and that the body is built as a house (Eph. 4:12, 16). Paul does not treat the concepts of family/fellowship and house/dwelling of God separately, but as bonded together, especially when he portrays the church as the planting of God (1 Cor. 3:6; 2 Cor. 9:10; Eph. 4:15, 16; Col. 2:19).

6.4.2   The Church as Edifice

Metaphors such as "house," "temple," and "building" express the idea of upbuilding. "Planting," "field" and others represent the concept of growth. They constitute a further definition of the Church as the people of God, in a similar way to the metaphor of the "body of Christ."

The Church is the temple of God (1 Cor. 3:16, 17; 2 Cor. 6:16; Eph. 2:21) and the indwelling of God (Rom. 8:9-11; 1 Cor. 3:16; Eph. 2:21; 2 Tim. 1:14; cf. Eph. 3:17; Rom. 8:10). This upbuilding must be seen as the continuing work of God with His people. There are two dimensions in this work: one is the bringing in of the non-believers, or conversion of sinners (Rom. 15:20ff.). The other is the inner strengthening and perfecting of all the believers, or the cleansing of the Church (1 Cor. 14:3; 1 Thess. 5:11).

Christ is the foundation of the building (1 Cor. 3:10) and apostles and prophets are ordained by him to that end (Eph. 2:20, 21; cf. Rom. 15:20). On this foundation, the Church is built up (Col. 2:7) and reaches adulthood, safeguarded and cleansed from all alien powers and doctrine (Eph. 4:12; Col. 2:6-8). God equips the Church with all sorts of gifts and powers and with various kinds of ministries for the sake of this upbuilding (Eph. 4:11ff.; 2 Cor. 10:8, 13:10; cf. Rom. 12:3, 6ff.; 1 Cor. 12:4ff., 28ff.). This upbuilding is most closely bound up with the proclamation of the Word of God in the world (1 Cor. 14:3; Rom. 15:20).

6.4.3   Contextuality of the Church

Gilliland points out that in systematizing Paul's doctrine for the Church universal, theologians have failed to see the contextual presuppositions of Paul. The way Paul applied the essence of Christian truth was appropriate to the nature of the cultural and human environment of each local congregation. Gilliland believes that this contextual aspect is part of the reason Paul's churches survived under immense pressure, growing in each place and multiplying among the unevangelized.

> Christianity was vibrant and alive because each local church found its own expression of the Christian life while at the same time it was joined in faith and truth to all other congregations that were also under Christ's lordship. (Gilliland, 1983:209)

Until the third century, there is no evidence of special buildings constructed for Christian gatherings. Paul's

121

churches were house churches in almost every case. Banks (1988:41) supposes that the number of people in attendance at meetings could have been around thirty, because of limitations of space. It is easy to imagine that in these scattered small churches people would have shared their similar lives and related naturally with each other, and also met the particular needs arising from a common socio-cultural context. They found their own expression of the Christian life with contextualized forms and styles.

This contextuality is crucial in upbuilding the Church. If Paul's churches had joined the church in Jerusalem and imported its forms and styles as their norm, they would have lost their independence, flexibility and vitality. Unity in diversity—in other words, contextual quality with basic commitment to their unique Lord—was the key to the extensive and intensive upbuilding of Paul's churches.

6.5 Summary

Pauline ecclesiology can be characterized in terms of both redemptive-historical aspects and christological aspects. The former refers to Paul's perspective of the Church as continuation and fulfillment of the Old Testament. He takes over the basic idea of the people of Israel and, to some extent, redefines it as the eschatological Israel. They are delivered from slavery to freedom and live as Christ's dedicated people in the world.

The latter aspect is the christological perspective. When Paul describes the Church as the "body of Christ," he presents this relationship two ways: the Church as one body (in Romans and 1 Corinthians), and the spiritual connection between Christ as Head and his Church, together with

Christ's all-embracing significance as the Head of all things (in Ephesians and Colossians).

Paul discusses the practice and upbuilding of the Church. The Church is expected to grow up unto Christ in maturity, as well as numerically. He describes the Church as the family of God wherein the community life conveys a dynamic appeal to the people. Paul also expresses the Church as an edifice wherein the unbeliever's conversion and the believer's perfecting take place. One of the reasons for the growth of Paul's churches can be traced to their contextuality. These Pauline notions of the church provide the foundation to develop the ethno-ecclesiology for Japan.

What does the Pauline ecclesiology mean in the context of Japan? We will develop an ethno-ecclesiology for Japan in chapter 9 and discuss it thoroughly. However, we briefly mention here that Japanese missiologists may have a good resource in Pauline ecclesiology with which to construct their own ecclesiology, one both faithful to the Biblical text and relevant to the Japanese context. In particular, power issues and solidarity issues in Pauline congregations provide us with some important missiological implications.

Now we turn to contemporary ecclesiology. This we cannot neglect, even if we could succeed at entering into a relationship both with the text and with the context. Importing Western theology brings with it the potential for miscommunicating the Christian witnesses. Yet to disregard it would cause us to miss blessings from God that we could share with Western people.

123

Chapter 7

Contemporary Ecclesiology

The aim of this chapter is to survey contemporary ecclesiology from a missiological perspective. The framework of this study follows that of Karl Barth, who develops his ecclesiology in three phases. He discusses the Church as instituted by God in the section on "The Holy Spirit and the Gathering of the Christian Community" (CD, IV/1/62) while the community aspect of the Church is treated in the section on "The Holy Spirit and Upbuilding of the Christian community." (CD, IV/2/67) The "orientation to the world" dimension of the Church is introduced in the section on "The Holy Spirit and the Sending of the Christian Community." (CD, IV/3/72)

Although Barth's division and structure are employed, the order of the following discussion differs from his. In the first two sections, we discuss the twofold character of the Church, the community aspect first and the institutional second. The reason will be given later. Finally, we will look at the Church's mediating function between Christ and his people.

7.1 Church as Organism

Hendrikus Berkhof focuses on the mediating function of the Church, concluding that the first task of the Church is to confront humanity with Christ. He writes,

> She [the Church] must be a place, a space, a home, where man is welcomed and led to Christ, where he is nourished, shaped, and renewed. But the consequence of that is that in this house there begins to grow a community of the renewed, people who have become mature through the gracious gifts (charismata) with which the Spirit equips them and which he wants them to use for the upbuilding of the community. (Berkhof, 1986:347)

Thus Berkhof puts the Church's institutional aspect first. Calvin sees the Church as a mother who brings forth the believers. For him, the Church's sense of community is its second aspect, since it is the purpose and fruit of the first.

As Van Engen points out, the Christian community needs to be visualized "as simultaneously a human organization and a divinely created organism. Its mission then is both gift and task, both spiritual and social." (Van Engen, 1991:35) However, from my Japanese person-oriented perspective, the order of Berkhof's ecclesiology cannot be accepted. The

Church's face as organism must be discussed first. If one acknowledges the word of Jesus that "where two or three come together in my name, I am there with them" (Matthew 18:20) as the essence of the church, and if Pentecost is the inauguration of the Church by the Holy Spirit, one must begin with the community.

The Holy Spirit created fellowship, assembling many separate individuals into a unity, a single "body." The essence of the Church is the Body of Christ, which is an effectual reality of a supra-logical kind, quasi-physical, and in any event, essentially organic. It is the oneness of communion with Christ by faith and the brotherhood of love.

Brunner expresses this idea by using the biblical word *ekklesia*, which is a true brotherhood in Christ. Although his usage of this word is an idealized one, we need to ask ourselves if we can talk about the future of the church without the inclination of seeking its future, its ideal, its utopia as a guide for values to be sought in the present. (See Zahrnt 1966.) He believes that the mission of the Gospel would be better served if the true *ekklesia* were more evident, (Brunner, 1952:108) and calls the Church to engage humankind with personal truth by an existential encounter. He consistently explains reality and Scripture in accordance with the motif of the priority of the personal over the impersonal. (1964:87, 102) This organic dimension of the Church needs to be supported by those who try to attract people toward Christ by involvement in their lives or by demonstrations of love. Brunner's intention is to carefully resist the understanding of the Church as a non-personal institution, an understanding which has been based on objectivism, in order to maintain the sense of a vital relationship between God and His people.

Thus if communion with Christ and the communion of the saints is the essence of the Church, how does this community aspect relate to the institutional aspect? Brunner explains that the existing institution of the Church should be understood as an instrument for the growth and renewal of the communion. The Church as system is an external mechanism for assisting the *ekklesia*, as a vessel to bring human beings into communion with the Lord Jesus Christ and to open their hearts to the needs of other believers. (See Brunner 1952:106–115.)

Although this explanation is acceptable, Brunner does not treat the organization of the church in sufficient detail. The reason he concentrates on the organism of the church is because of his pessimistic view of the institutional church. He actually follows Rudolph Sohm's antithesis to all law. (Brunner, 1952:107) Although in a sense he evaluates the meaning of the institution positively, his interests always focus on the problem of its essential function. Therefore, as Honecker points out, "the forms and order of the church are recognized as the problems of *ekklesia* which was corrupted into the institution." (Honecker, 1963:118) Brunner does not deal adequately with the concrete forms of the church.

7.2 Church as Organization

As Van Engen (1991:37) points out, until Bonhoeffer's work, most ecclesiology had involved an *a priori*, logical, scholastic thought process. Bonhoeffer's assumption is that the message of Christianity is not about abstractions but about actual life, not about humankind in general but about human beings facing the practical problems of their existence. Bonhoeffer's concern is shared by Barth when he discusses an earthly-historical form of the Christian community.

> The Christian community as such cannot exist as an ideal commune or *universum*, but—also in time and space—only in the relationship of its individual members as they are fused together by the common action of the Word which they have heard into a definite human fellowship; in concrete form, therefore, and visible to everyone. (Barth, 1956:653)

Bonhoeffer distinguishes two misunderstandings of the Church. First, there is a historical misunderstanding, in which the Church is confused with the religious community. Here, the reality of the new primary relationships, which are ordained by God and lie beyond all "religious motives" leading to empirical fellowship, is overlooked. Second, there is a religious misunderstanding, in which the Church is confused with the Kingdom of God, and man's historical restriction is not taken seriously. Neither of these misunderstandings take seriously the reality of the Church, which is simultaneously a historical fellowship and God-established reality.

In *Sanctorum Communio* ("The Communion of Saints"), Bonhoeffer explains that the insights of social philosophy and sociology can be fruitful for Christian dogmatic thinking about the concept of the Church. He considers the relation between the human social community and the divine spiritual community by introducing a sociological perspective into the existing theological one.

His conviction about God, who has become in Jesus a God for people in the context of social existence, led him to write the following sentences from a Nazi prison in 1944: "The church is the church only when it exists for others... The church must share in the secular problems of ordinary human life, not dominating, but helping and serving." (Bonhoeffer, 1971:382) Bonhoeffer presented a new perspective of Church as being *for the world*, a concept which will be treated in the next section.

Therefore, the institutional Church must be a structured community—and, at the same time, a spiritual community. The Church is the God-established, Christ-directed and Spirit-animated institution of salvation. It includes institutional elements, such as instruction, office, order, sacraments, preaching, teaching, worship, and the like.

Barth's view of the Church as being an event provides a way to abandon the distinctions between community and institution. "Its act is its being, its status its dynamic, essence and existence." (Barth, 1956:650) When the event that is Church takes place, God allows certain people to live as His witnesses of reconciliation between the world and Himself. The Church exists in the form of a sequence and nexus of definite human activities. The community is the earthly-historical form of existence of Jesus Christ Himself. It is his body created and continually renewed by the awakening power of the Holy Spirit. (Barth, 1961)

Moltmann expresses the Church as being in the process of renewal, as follows: "The church is on the move in free solidarity and critical fellowship, together with the world, people and peoples, nations and societies." (1977:1) It can be said that some contemporary theologians view the Church as one which is emerging toward the full manifestation of its true nature.

Comparing Barth's view of the Church to Brunner's, it might be concluded that Brunner's concept of *ekklesia* is so idealized that it can hardly be recognized in real life. (See Barth 1958:616.) Although all churches need to hear his intention to fight against the lifeless institutionalization of the Church, at the same time, the Church's institutional aspect cannot be ignored. The Christian community can exist only in a time-space reality, and therefore it takes place among humanity in the form of human activity. Brunner is too pessimistic about the instituted church, so his division between content and vessel faces the danger of ecclesiastical docetism.

Brunner's spiritualized, idealized *"ekklesia"* had little connection to reality. But Japanese churches today suffer something similar, in having little contextual grounding in Japanese culture. Ken Ishihara critically analyzes the history of Christianity in Japan:

The modernization of Japan in the Meiji era closely paralleled its Westernization and, therefore the two were indistinguishable. What this caused was a virtual romanticing of Christianity that stood as a curious, isolated artifact on the Japanese landscape. I think that from the Meiji era to the Taisho era, while Christianity was introduced and was facilitating people's yearning toward the West, Christian theology did not have an *Apologetik*. Lacking a viable mechanism to deliver its theology in terms of Japanese culture, the system could not effectively be grafted into the predominant thinking of the masses. Left to its own, for example, Christianity

> failed totally in its ability to relate to Shinto or
> the indigenous culture. (Ishihara, 1976:88–89)

We need to see both the community aspect and institutional aspect of the church to contextualize the Christian
church in Japan's context.

7.3 Being for the World

Bosch (1991:389) rightly evaluates Barth as one of the first
theologians to articulate mission as an activity of God Himself.
Barth insists that the community of believers must be strongly
focused on the ministry of Christ. He sees that the existence
and task of the Christian community lies in the witness of Jesus
Christ in the face of the whole world, to summoning it to faith
in Him.

> The community of Jesus Christ is itself creature
> and therefore world. Hence, as it exists for men
> and the world, it also exists for itself. But it is the
> human creature which is ordained by nature to
> exist for the other human creatures distinct from
> it... Even within the world to which it belongs.
> It does not exist ecstatically or eccentrically with
> reference to itself, but wholly with reference to
> them, to the world around. It saves and maintains
> its own life as it interposes and gives itself for all
> other human creatures. (Barth, 1962:762)

Bonhoeffer's letter from a Nazi prison is along the same
lines: "The Church is the Church only when it exists for
others." (1971:203)

The Church participates in Christ's Messianic mission and in the creative mission of the Spirit. Therefore, Moltmann calls for a look outward to the world in which the Church is to be the Church. "The church does not stay in social isolation but becomes a living hope in the midst of the people." (1977:xvi) The Church is called the wayfaring people: "At the same time it stands before God in fellowship and solidarity with all men and is bound to send up to him out of the depths the common cry for life and liberty." (1977:1)

Moltmann asserts that what makes the Church the Church is reconciliation "in the blood of Christ," and its own self-giving for the reconciliation of the world. Therefore, the Church of Christ is at the same time "the Church under the cross." The fellowship of Christ is experienced wherever Christians take up their cross on themselves. This fellowship is experienced through common resistance to idolatry and inhumanity, and in common suffering. (1977:97) He quotes Matthew 25:31–46, and introduces it into his ecclesiology; by doing so he emphasizes an identification with the oppressed on the basis of God's presence *per identificationem* with the least of men (p. 130). Moltmann's thesis of identification of the oppressed has been followed by Sobrino (1984), Segundo (1973), Boff (1986), and others.

Berkhof (1986:421) has summarized four activities of the Church in ministering to and drawing in people: 1) intercessory prayer, 2) witness, 3) the ministry of mercy, and 4) prophecy.

Hoekendijk's (1966:72) idea of the Church clearly shows its orientation to the world:

> Thus the church must prove her legitimacy, her "realness," by being there for the other. She does

133

> not exist in herself and certainly not for herself
> either; just as the Messiah did not exist in and
> for himself.

However, because of his strongly pessimistic view of the organized churches, he does not adequately treat the congregations themselves. For him, "the church has little more than the character of an 'intermezzo' between God and the world." (Bosch, 1991:384) This purely apostolary approach, together with the study group of the World Council of Churches, led to an orientation toward the political, and neglected the Church's own involvement in mission.

Other attempts to express a more holistic understanding of the Church than that of Hoekendijk include a "foretaste of the Kingdom" (Newbigin, 1953:147), "the provisional representation of the calling of all humanity and indeed of all creatures" (Barth, 1962:681), and "the experimental garden of a new humanity" (Berkhof, 1986:419).

In this discussion, Berkhof's emphasis on the Church's virtue of 'being different' is crucial. He writes,

> The church is not apostolary because and to
> the extent that she sacrifices her being-herself
> to being an instrument; rather it is precisely her
> being-herself that is to work in the world in an
> apostolary way. That can only be done if her
> being-in-the-world is a being-different-from-the-
> world. (1986:419)

When the Church's "orientation to the world" is discussed, we must consider both her being-different-from-the-world and her continuity with the world. On this integrated foundation, the Church's mediation functions to bridge the gap between Christ and the world by standing between them. The apostolic task can only be done if her being-in-the-world is a being-different-from-the-world. Berkhof's conviction is that the Church's unique nature as Spirit-guided community will gradually emerge toward its full manifestation to the world.

What does this mean in a Japanese ecclesiological context? Unfortunately there are high barriers between the NCC (National Council of Church) group and Evangelicals (including Charismatics). On the one hand, the NCC group emphasizes the Church's responsibility to the world and views the Church as a secondarily important reality; on the other hand, Evangelicals—in reaction to them—have become irrelevant to the world, and many churches have become introverted.

The majority of NCC churches focus on world affairs, such as the problem of the Emperor system, political or religious power systems that neglect human rights, dialogue with other religions, urban slums, discrimination of minorities, racism, depersonalization, war-guilt and the like. This, for them, is nearly the complete orbit of the Church's activity. The Church is no longer recognized as the locus of encounter between God and human; they follow the trend of the WCC and have established a new order of God's mission: God–world–church.

In a negative reaction against the NCC churches, most Evangelicals have not attempted to touch upon these agenda. They concentrate on 'being different' from the world and, intentionally or unintentionally, have condemned the world as pagan. According to their perspective, the Church is the 'holy place' and the world is the 'polluted place,' and so their

135

prime attitude toward the world has been to attempt to get away from it.

Thus, the NCC group have lost the Church, and the Evangelicals, in a sense, have lost the mission. Both of them need to reconsider God's intended ecclesiology for Japan. Actually, the direction which we are seeking to aim towards is not the middle of two extremes, but is rather the sound synthesis of Church and mission. "The concept of the Church as institution and the Church as missionary body are not alternatives, but simply two facets that must be held together in the reality of one Church." (Neill, 1957:23) Anderson (1992:75) writes,

> The church exists as the missionary people of God—that is its nature. The mission of the church is to embody in its corporate life and ministry, the continuing messianic and incarnational nature of the Son of God through the indwelling of the Holy Spirit. It is on this basis that I argue that the nature of the church is determined in its existence as the mission of God to the world.

A contextual ecclesiology in Japan will emerge when the existence of the Church is grasped as salt keeping the saltiness, scattered in the world. (Matthew 5:13) The Church is not intended to exist in a special capsule for Christians, shut off from the outer world. She is expected to function as a God-sending agency in the world for Christ, in the same way that salt functions only if it is scattered.

However, at the same time, another aspect that must be emphasized is that she is required to maintain her essence in

136

the world. If her quality is earthly, she is no use as a witness, just like salt is that has lost its saltness. The Church and world should be intimately related. The Church has to be proof and a model of God's intentions for the world. She is a Spirit-filled community for the sake of all humans.

7.4 Summary

The Church has been embraced by contemporary theologians primarily in three aspects. First, it is an organism in fellowship with other believers in and through Christ. The Church's essence is the oneness of communion with Christ by faith and brotherhood in love.

Second, it is an organization. The Christian community as such cannot exist as an ideal commune or *universum*, but must exist in time and space. The church is the God-established, Christ-directed and Spirit-animated institution of salvation. Therefore, from the point of view of seeing the Church as being an event, we can say that it is at the same time a spiritual community and a structured institution.

The third aspect of the Church is its orientation to the world. The church stands between Christ and the world, and exercises a mediating function. This apostolic task can only be done if her being-in-the-world is a being-different-from-the-world.

Chapter 8

Premises of Ethno-Ecclesiology

How can we deal with Pauline ecclesiology and contemporary Western ecclesiology in order to construct the image and the concept of the church for the Japanese people? Before we ask this question, we need to treat some premises: 1) the reason why we discuss ethno-ecclesiology, 2) the relationship between contextualization and empowerment, and 3) the way that the Japanese view the Church. Based on these premises, we will try to establish in the next chapter an ethno-ecclesiology for Japan.

8.1 Why Ethno-ecclesiology?

One of the major reasons for the stagnation of Japanese churches is a lack of contextualization, and as Padilla (1985:107) asserts, "the contextualization of the gospel can never take place apart from the contextualization of the church."

8.1.1 God's Attitude toward Culture

Kraft (1979) discusses the relationship between God and culture, consulting Niebuhr's (1951) three basic positions. We treat two of these positions here and set our focus on how to grapple with God's view of the Japanese culture.

One position is called the "God-against-culture position." For those who take the position that God is opposed to culture, the choice for commitment to God is by definition a decision to oppose culture, which is thought to be in the power of Satan. The recommendation that advocates of the "God-against-culture position" typically give is for Christians to withdraw, reject, escape, isolate, and insulate themselves from the world in order to develop and maintain holiness.

Kraft points out that this approach makes some serious errors. The advocates of this position do not understand the characteristics of culture, in particular that their culture is within them as well as around them so it is impossible to escape from it—but that it is possible to innovate, replace, add to or transform it. They assume that all culture is evil, while overlooking the fact that what God stands against is allegiance to the Satanic use of culture, not to the culture itself. Kraft insists that the Christian way is to pledge allegiance to God and use culture for Him.

Identifying Japanese culture as essentially heathen in terms of the "God-against-culture position" has brought damaging results in Christian communication. Unfortunately this idea was imported unconsciously by some missionaries who hold a "God-endorsing-my-culture perspective," and has been continued by some Japanese church leaders. They equated Western culture with Christian culture, and adopted a confrontational stance toward Japanese culture. New converts were encouraged to disassociate themselves from their own culture and were prohibited from participating in most of the social functions of Japanese society. As a result, they broke the natural social relationships they had with the majority of Japanese and lost all points of contact for communicating the Christian message.

Another position is the "God-above-but-through-culture position." This model assumes that, although God exists totally outside of culture while humans exist totally within culture, He chooses to use culture as the vehicle for interaction with human beings. Kraft sees culture as a kind of roadmap made up of various forms designed to get people where they need to go. "These forms and the functions they are intended to serve are seen, with few exceptions, as neutral with respect to the interaction between God and man." (1979:113) For Kraft, culture is seen neither as inherently evil or inherently good, but as the arena of God's interaction with people. Human culture can be viewed primarily as a vehicle to be used by the communicators for Christian purposes, rather than as an enemy to be combatted or shunned.

We take this "God-above-but-through-culture position" to develop our ecclesiology. This stance is both Biblically sound and practically effective. If Jesus lived as a human being in Japan today, would he shut himself in a holy, uncontaminated place as defined by advocates of the "God-against-Japanese-culture" position? No, he would participate in the midst of real life situations to communicate the Gospel at our level. In spite of the limitations and flaws of current

141

Japanese culture, he would freely choose to employ Japanese culture and at major points to limit himself to the capacities of the culture in his interaction with Japanese people.

8.1.2 Contextualization

The "God-above-but-through-culture position" opens the door for the Church to utilize to its advantage Japanese indigenous cultural forms, as this position sees the forms of culture as essentially neutral. The employing of indigenous cultural forms for Christian purposes by fulfilling indigenous functions to convey through them Christian meanings is called "contextualization."

The term "contextualization" has been widely debated among Evangelicals, but their attitude toward it has changed and in general Evangelicals have begun to identify contextualization as a vital requirement for missions today. For the sake of understanding better the gospel of incarnation, the Japanese church, as members of the body of Christ, interpret the Word, using their own thoughts and employing their own cultural gifts. (Gilliland, 1989:12–13)

Kraft explains the same concept using his term, "a dynamic-equivalence church."

> A dynamic-equivalence church produces an impact on the people of the society of which it is a part equivalent to that which the scripturally described peoples of God produced upon the original hearers. In that equivalence the church will need leadership, organization, education, worship, buildings, behavioral standards, and

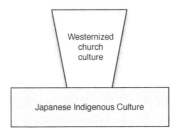

Figure 18: Japanese Christianity as a Potted Plant

means of expressing Christian love and concern to the people of its own culture who have not yet responded to Christ. But a dynamically equivalent church will employ culturally appropriate forms in meeting these needs—familiar, meaningful forms that it will possess, adapt, and fill with Christian meanings. (Kraft, 1979:321)

The key to evangelizing Japan and raising up a powerful missionary force lies in multiplying dynamic, culturally relevant churches. Japanese Christianity is like a "potted plant" which has been transported without having been transplanted. (See Conn 1984:246.) Japanese churches have been highly Westernized and they have not dealt sufficiently with traditional Japanese cultural systems. As the result of uncritical rejection, labeling unique Japanese cultural forms as "pagan", most Japanese have identified Christianity as a foreign religion to which they do not have to relate.

For effective Christian communication, communicators need to convey God's message while at the same time paying attention to the context, and especially to the religions that have functioned to serving the felt needs of the people. Communicators use the forms of the local culture, but they transform them into tools for the expression of the Christian faith. Employing and transforming Japanese religious forms for Christian purposes is a better alternative than using Western church forms, which have not worked particularly well thus far as vehicles of communication. The purpose of contextualization is to have an indigenous church using indigenous forms to which are attached Christian meanings, so that people will think of the Lord as their own God who meets their needs within the context of their own society and culture. In every step of our communicational strategy, we need to be reminded that it is the communicator who must change his/her patterns to fit the cultural context of his/her receptor.

We need an ethno-ecclesiology and a contextualized model of church for Japan for three reasons: Firstly, God, who loves diversity, desires to receive a particularly Japanese expression of love and praise to Him in His Church; second, God intends to communicate His love and will do so through the contextualized church, using the gift of Japanese culture as a vehicle; and third, God has decided to bless the universal Church through a uniquely Japanese way of living out the Gospel and understanding the church. God's mountain (the biblical data) needs to be drilled not only in a Western mine shaft (Western cultural perspective), but also in Japanese mine shafts and the six thousand or more other cultural mine shafts. (See Kraft 1979:33.)

> The contextualization of the gospel can only
> be a gift of grace granted by God to a church
> that is seeking to place the totality of life under

144

the Lordship of Christ in its historical situation.
(Padilla, 1985:109)

8.2 Contextualization and Empowerment

Although contextualization is a "must" for evangelizing
Japanese people, can we employ all cultural forms for Christian
ends? Can we contextualize the cultural forms of Japanese
religions even when we know that they were empowered by the
enemy? Is there any possibility of bringing confusion or mis-
communication as a result of using the indigenous religion's
forms? The aim of this section is to clarify the relationship
between contextualization issues and empowerment issues
and seek ways to integrate them into a holistic Christian
approach.

8.2.1 The Enemy Uses Cultural Forms

Although Creation was designed to declare the glory of God
(Psalm 19; Warner 1991:32), Satan tries to, and to some extent
has, put Creation under his control to frustrate the plan of
God. His intention is to carry on his war against God through
the created order. He has tried to mar the reflection of God's
glory in nature by introducing enmity, perversion, and even
catastrophe into this realm (Romans 8:18–19).

The Bible refers to Satan in various ways. He is "the god of
this age" (2 Cor. 4:4), "the blinder" (2 Cor. 4:4), "the prince of
this world" (John 14:30; 16:11), "the ruler of the kingdom of
the air" (Eph 2:1-2), and the like. His authority is not absolute,

even though he wields all kinds of destructive influence over all levels of life and exerts his greatest hostility against God's redemptive purpose.

> While God is ultimately sovereign, since he is the creator of everything that exists, Satan has been allowed to exercise a great amount of evil activity on the earth. (Arnold, 1992:93)

As White (1990:33) asserts, Dualism was foreign to biblical theologies. God is supreme over all created beings including demons and evil spirits. Satan exercises only the power that God permits. "The earth is the Lord's, and all its fullness" (1 Cor. 10:26, 28).

What is the relationship between demonic power and physical objects? In 1 Corinthians 8–10, Paul deals with the issue of eating meat offered to idols. One of the central features of his argument is that there is a demonic character to non-Christian religions. He insists that an idol has no real, independent existence (8:4). But at the same time he recognizes that there is a close connection between idolatry and demonic activity. There is a supernatural power associated with idols that resides in demons (10:19–20). Wagner (1992:79) concludes that "there is a pernicious relationship between demonic beings and physical objects, even though the objects in themselves are only wood or metal or stone or plastic or whatever."

There is good reason to assume that the cultural forms of Shinto, Buddhism, and New Religions have the potential for incredibly malignant power. If demons can and do attach themselves to material objects, how can we employ them for Christian witness?

146

8.2.2   Blessing, Cursing and Renouncing

A Christian communicator can exercise God's authority over "all the power of the enemy" (Luke 10:19). Jesus delegated authority to his disciples to act as ambassadors, and to do the works of ministry that he did (Luke 10:17–20; John 14:12). Jesus prayed to his father, "As you sent me into the world, I have sent them into the world" (John 17:18). Ephesians 3:10 indicates that God has chosen to reveal his redemptive plan to the rulers and authorities in the heavenly realms through the Church.

Therefore we can renounce the influence of spiritual activity that is behind occult objects in the name of the Lord Jesus Christ. We can renounce the curse of the enemy on the cultural forms of the Japanese religions by the authority of Jesus, thereby commanding any demons enforcing the curse to go to the Cross to make their claim.

After such a renouncing, is it no longer a problem to use these forms for Christian communication? There may be three options for dealing with these cultural forms: 1) destroy them; 2) not destroy and not use them for Christian ends; 3) not destroy but use them for Christian ends.

When objects are made for occult purposes, such as *omamori* (amulets), *ofuda* (charms), *ema* (prayer tablets), *butsudan* (Buddhist house altar), *kamidana* (Shinto high shelf) and *haraigushi* (a sacred tree for Shinto purification rites), the only appropriate way to deal with them is to destroy them. Even though the value of the material destroyed may be very great, we should not hesitate in this matter. (Prince, 1990:70–71) points out that books can be channels of occult power, quoting the burning of the scrolls related to sorcery in

Acts 19. Warner (1991:122) interprets the same event in terms of a power encounter. "This is not only symbolic of one's break with such practices; it is an open challenge to the demonic powers behind them to defend themselves if they can." In some cases, we may expect such a power encounter when we destroy the occult objects.

When the object has not been made for occult purposes, we should then decide whether or not to contextualize it. When people look to an object with the anticipation that it has power, demons will meet their expectation quite apart from any qualities inherent in the object itself. Alternatively, in other cases, a person engaging in occult practices may invite demons to empower an object, and in this way the demons may become associated with that object. (Warner, 1991:93) In these cases, there is no spiritual problem after we break the power of the demons behind the objects, in Jesus' name, and forbid them to return to the object. At this point, the only problem we should consider is the communicational one. After renouncing the demonic influences, we need to adapt and employ them to serve Christian ends, evaluating them as to whether or not they can both fulfil their indigenous functions and also convey a Christian meaning.

Before moving to the next chapter, we briefly mention God's blessing on cultural forms—including words, material objects, and places. Several illustrations of God's empowerment on cultural forms are found in Scripture: anointing oil (James 5:14), Paul's handkerchiefs and aprons (Acts 19:12), Peter's shadow (Acts 5:15), and Jesus' garment (Luke 8:44). If Satanic power can reside in cultural forms, how much more powerfully can the almighty God empower them! We can take God's authority over the demons and both speak

148

against them and bless cultural forms in Jesus' name. (See Kraft 1989:161–163.)

8.2.3   Redemptive Gift

John Dawson believes that God intends each city to be a place of shelter, a place of communion, and a place of personal liberation, even though many Christians think of cities to be, by nature, evil places. He writes, "I believe our cities have the mark of God's sovereign purpose upon them. Our cities contain what I call a redemptive gift." (Dawson, 1989:39)

Just as God sees a sinful person in spite of his/her miserable situation, so He sees cities despite their poverty, cruelty and violence. He not only accepts them but also shares his redemptive plan. If one fixes one's eyes on God's plan for cities and identifies that plan, one can be optimistic of the future of our cities, despite their current hopeless condition. This conviction is based on the fact that only God is the Creator and He has created all things for His glory. "Satan is not a creator. He cannot originate anything. He can only turn created things and people to his own purposes." (Dawson, 1989:41) The task of Christian communicators is to restore the redemptive gift of the cities by fighting against the enemy.

In the same way, Jacobs (1992) tries to identify the redemptive plan for nations. For example, she sees Japan's gift as restoration, the United States' as the authority of the believer, Israel's as the attribute of God, England's as the majesty of God, Korea's as prayer, and the like. These analyses need to be evaluated cautiously. However, we agree with her proposition that God desires the nations and the people of the nations to be part of the Kingdom of God.

149

The same logic of this concept of a redemptive gift for nations and cities can be applied to the cultural forms of the Japanese religions. As discussed above, we know that there are spiritual influences or curses of the enemy behind them. Some of the redemptive gifts of these religious forms have been turned to the enemy's use, but we believe that God expects his children to restore the original purpose of the redemptive gifts for Him, because they were created for His glory.

We begin contextualizing each cultural form by identifying its redemptive gift, on the basis of the understanding that it is essentially neutral, renouncing the enemy's power, and then empowering it by the mighty name of Jesus Christ.

8.3 Image or Concept

Taber (1978) points out that the Western theologian used intellectual tools, neo-Platonism, Aristotelianism, scholasticism in its various forms, down to contemporary existentialism, phenomenology, process philosophy, and linguistic philosophy—all of which are highly abstract cognitive concepts. Abstractness is a valuable tool for generalizing from the concrete and particular—but it loses greatly in terms of dynamic impact upon persons, especially upon the non-specialist.

Taber introduces two terms, 'concept' and 'mental image', and distinguishes between them to analyse what Western theologians have used and what they have ignored. Taber writes,

> It will be seen that concept relates closely to what I have said about technical language; it is

very powerful for analysis, but extremely weak in affective impact. Image, on the other hand, is much more specific but much less precise. Its boundaries are vague. Whereas a concept is peculiarly my own, and therefore closely bound up with my attitudes and my motivations. The difference can be clearly seen by contrasting the concept "dog" in English, which is defined in terms of sufficient and necessary components of meaning, and the image I have in my brain of *my* dog.

On the whole, it is fair to say, the Bible deals in images rather than in concepts, especially in describing the ineffable. (1978:6)

Concept	Mental Image
Abstract	Concrete
General/Universal	Specific/particular
Analytical	Holistic/*Gestalt*
Linear	Multi-dimensional
Rational	Affective
Evokes cognitive knowledge	Evokes intuitive knowledge
Sharply narrowing focus	Broadly evocative focus
Univocal	Multiple layers of meaning

Table 6: Two Categories For Theologizing (Taber, 1978:6)

Song (1986) asserts that Asian culture is shaped by the power to think in terms of images and not by the capacity to conceptualize. He thinks that Asian culture is vibrant with the rhythms of life that cannot be abstracted into definitions, logic and formulas. He encourages theologians in Asia to focus

151

on the theological core of life—the innermost recesses of the human heart where a person senses God and struggles with God—and to use this 'echo from the core,' transcribing it into theology. We need to touch the 'core of being' where the Japanese and God meet in search of the meaning of life.

> This power of imaging must be the energy that enables us to do theology. And what is most important, this must be the power making us image theology and not conceptualize it, hear theology and not theorize about it, see theology and not turn it into a mechanism for argumentation. (Song, 1986:64)

In spite of the actual difference in context, Japanese people still have a certain commonality in their deep worldview level with other Asian people. We believe Song's approach is meaningful for Japanese theologians, too. As Schreiter (1986:31) recommends, Japanese theology may be done via poetry.

Lingenfelter and Mayers (1986) try to explain Western culture and non-Western culture quoting the "Dual-Brain Theory" of Baken (1971) and Cohen (1969). Westerners, with a dominant left hemisphere, may often think largely in the verbal or language mode, whereas non-Western people, with a dominant right hemisphere, may often think largely in concrete images or the signal-pictorial mode.

Lingenfelter and Mayers contend that as Jesus taught he utilized right-hemisphere, pictorial, concrete, holistic, and analogic strategies rather than left-hemisphere, verbal, abstract, dichotomistic, and analytic thought. Jesus presents his message with one powerful image after another, using illustrations

Left Hemisphere	Right Hemisphere
verbal	signal-pictorial
rational	emotional
analytic (dichotomistic)	synthetic (holistic)
digital	analogical

Table 7: Dual Brain Theory (Lingenfelter and Mayers, 1986:58)

from nature, tradition, and daily life. His communication is receptor-oriented, focusing on the people who are receiving the communication and on the cultural factors that will affect their understanding of it. He knew that his receptors were image-oriented. "Jesus preached his message to the people, using many other parables like these; he told them as much as they could understand." (Mark 4:33)

How should we go about ethno-ecclesiology for Japan? Must we use a right-hemisphere or a left-hemisphere approach? Are our receptors image-oriented? The answer is "yes and no." One thing we can say is that a split brain is a malfunctioning brain. That is, two separate brains would tend to contradict each other, rather than work as an integrated unit. Neither concept-oriented ecclesiology, such as Küng's *The Church* (1976) and Berkouwer's *The Church* (1976), nor image-oriented ecclesiology, such as Miner's *Images of the Church in the New Testament* (1960) and Dulles' *Models of the Church*, (1974) will work in the Japanese context.

In fact, image is not different from concept. When the Apostle Paul refers to the Church as the "body of Christ," although the expression itself is an image, it conveys many concepts, such as unity among believers, Head-body solidarity, the church as Christ's fullness, and the like. Barth seems to succeed in integrating image and concept in his ecclesiology when he points to the Church as being an event (CD 4/1).

Therefore, we will seek to explain the Church in terms of questions emerging from the Japanese context, in conjunction with Pauline ecclesiology, consulting contemporary ecclesiology.

8.4 Summary

We take the "God-above-but-through-culture" position to develop our ethno-ecclesiology. Although God exists totally outside of culture, He chooses to use Japanese culture as the vehicle for interaction with human beings. In spite of the limitations and flaws of the current Japanese culture, God would freely choose to utilize it. Since this position sees the forms of culture as essentially neutral, it opens the door for contextualization of the Church. The employing of indigenous cultural forms to serve Christian ends by fulfilling indigenous functions to convey through them Christian meanings is called contextualization.

Although contextualization is a vital requirement for missions today, we cannot employ all cultural forms for Christian ends. We see a demonic character to non-Christian religions and pernicious relationships between demons and physical objects. When the objects are made for occult purposes, we should destroy them. When the objects are not made for occult purposes, we need to deal with both spiritual problems and communicational problems. In Jesus' name, we can break the power of the demons behind the objects. After renouncing the demonic influences, if we evaluate the objects and determine that we can fulfill their indigenous functions and still convey Christian meaning through them, we can employ them for Christian purposes. We begin contextualizing each cultural form by identifying its redemptive gift, renouncing the enemy's power, and empowering it by the mighty name of Jesus Christ.

Japanese, as non-Western people, often think largely in concrete images or the signal-pictorial mode, whereas Westerners may often think largely in the verbal or language mode. In constructing our ethno-ecclesiology, we designate a couple of *images* of the Church and from those images, we decode some *concepts* of the Church. We try to integrate image and concept in our ecclesiology in the next chapter.

Chapter 9

Ethno-Ecclesiology Applied to Japan

At this point, we need to review the Japanese questions examined in the previous part: 1) "Who gives us life-giving power?", 2) "Who protects us?", 3) "To whom or to what do I belong?", and 4) "How can I reach eternity?" These questions need to be answered by a contextualized Church. We will designate two images of the Church—"divine family" and "holy place"—for our Japanese ethno-ecclesiology.

9.1 Divine Family

We first discuss the image of "divine family," which represents the community aspect of the Church. The institutional aspect will be treated in the next section. The image of divine family conveys at least three concepts: empowered people, living communion, and family enterprise.

9.1.1   Empowered People: Children of *kami*

Shaw (1981) researches the Samo culture and presents a unique Christian role in that society. He insists that every Christian has access to God's supernatural power and acts as a priest who cares about the fears people have and assists them in interacting with the powerful Christ who gives "new life." There are at least two questions we should ask concerning this presentation: firstly, is it Biblical? Secondly, is it applicable to Japanese Christians?

A certain commonality can be found between the Colossians, the Samo, and the Japanese. They seek an answer to their crises in the spiritual realms. The Colossians found themselves in a slavish position of subjugation to the powers and principalities. The Samo feel a need for power that can protect them against the cursing of their lands, sorcery, and illness. The Japanese have a fundamental fear that malevolent spirits might damage their living. It is believed that an unhappy spirit, who has not been properly cared for, causes hindrances and problems to its living kin. These three kinds of people represent those who are struggling with the influence of the powers of darkness.

Paul never denies the existence and activities of angelic powers in heaven and on earth, both in their subjection to and in their rebelliousness against God. Paul had a clear image of the role of the Church in spiritual warfare.

> The church traces its origins and its vital energies to strategic events in heaven, where God has declared war on his Satanic Majesty and has demonstrated the mode and tools of final victory. (Miner, 1959:47)

Paul's prescription for this problem of Colossians can be our model, and it can be accurately applied in the context of Japan. He intended to dissuade the Colossians from continuing to fear the influence of the demonic powers in their lives by reminding them of their identification with Christ in his death and resurrection. They were buried with Christ and raised with him through their faith in God's power (Col. 2:12). Paul admonished them to regard themselves as dead to the evil powers (Col. 2:20) and alive to Christ because they had been raised with him. (Col. 3:1). For because they died, their life is now hidden with Christ in God (Col. 3:3). "Becoming a Christian means being linked to a powerful Lord who wields overpowering authority over the realm of darkness." (Arnold, 1992:116)

Paul's strategy is receptor-oriented. He knew the Colossian questions and tried to enter into their frame of references to communicate his message. Van Rheenen correctly describes the Christian strategy in an animistic context.

> In an animistic context the message must center on the cosmic conflict between God and the gods, between Christ and the demons, between the church and the principalities and powers. Christ's kingdom confronts the kingdom of Satan, and in the cross Christ has already become victorious over the domain of Satan. (Van Rheenen, 1991:61)

Shaw's "every person a priest" model is both biblical and applicable to Japan's context. As Hanson (1986:469) concludes, "the biblical notion of community was born out of the experience of having been delivered from slavery to freedom."

159

In Japan's highly animistic context, the community, whose members were delivered from slavery by malevolent deities to freedom of Christ, will really appeal to the Japanese people. The Christian community lives in communion with the risen Lord through the experience of the Holy Spirit. The people of God in Japan are protected from any influence of evil power because of Jesus who has the power of resurrection. They are a visible manifestation of the spiritual commonwealth on account of the constant presence of Jesus Christ who reigns in his supreme power over the malevolent spirits.

The Japanese, with Paul, need to view Christ as the One who is victorious over the powers. Christ is the Head of all things, superior to all principalities and powers, and he fills all things. Since Japanese *kami* sometimes represent a life force, a source and manifestation of energy found in the world, we may define Christ as Great *kami*. We can introduce Christ as the Head of the universe, who rules over the various deities and blesses Japanese life with life-giving power.

The concept of *kami* or 'children of *kami*' contains a rich series of meanings, one of which would be 'superhuman.' Because of a sense of continuity between *kami* and human beings, human beings who had some extraordinary quality, as well as other people, such as emperors, heroes, *uji* (family ancestors), and the like are referred to as *kami*. They are acknowledged as those who interact with supernatural beings; in other words, they are empowered people selected from the world. In this sense, Christians can be defined as children of *kami*—people who share the common attribute with *kami*—because of their interaction with a supernatural being.

The Church in Japan is the empowered people of God, and we may call them the children of *kami*. They are identified with Christ in his death and resurrection, and ordained by Christ, the Great *kami*. They are a divine family, and every family member has access to God's supernatural power and can apply His power of resurrection by reaching out in love to those who live in fear of spirits. They have attained to the royal priesthood, showing love and caring for the fears people have, bringing them to a point of interaction with the powerful Christ, who gives "new life."

9.1.2   Living Communion

In chapter three, we discussed the *amae* mentality. *Amae* is the desire to be at one emotionally with others who care for us, along with the emotion of enjoying this oneness. We point out that this denial of separation makes the Japanese group-oriented. A group provides a sense of belonging, peace of mind and identity for its members.

The Christian Church is able to provide warm fellowship in God's love, surrounded by care, and supported by a sense of identity. In creating community, God has graciously provided for deep-seated human needs, such as the needs for comfort, encouragement, and support. (See Hanson 1986:501.) As Gilliland (1983:187) insists, "fellowship among the people of God has to be planned and promoted as one of the highest priorities in mission work."

The notion of God's family indicates more than merely "warm fellowship." It provides a new identity for the Japanese people, who are themselves in the midst of an identity crisis. Christians are God's dearly loved adopted children whom He has made His heirs. This sense of being God's family constitutes their identity.

Modern urban inhabitants who have been uprooted from the traditional community are seeking a new sense of belonging. They will be drawn into a new community and hear the voice of God saying "I shall be your God, and you shall be my people." Thus they will identify themselves as the household of God.

Doi, who developed the concept of the *amae* mentality, discusses it in relationship to the Christian faith. (1990:154–168) He points out the similarity between *amae* and faith, and the superiority of faith to *amae*. As the needs of *amae* give rise to groupism when they are not fulfilled by human relationships, they become projected into the religious sphere. Doi insists that the danger for the Japanese is their inclination to be self-sufficient in their *amae*. Faith is often confused with *amae* because *amae* and faith overlap and exist side by side. Doi's analysis suggests that Jesus *allows* the humanistic *amae* mentality to abound. However, at the same time, he utilizes it to its fullest measure as a crucial step for developing the kind of intimacy in relationships that will move the Japanese toward an abiding faith.

Doi's study provides some crucial missiological implications: 1) *Amae* mentality will be a point of contact for the group-oriented Japanese people but it is not a goal of our witness. We need to challenge Japanese people to enter into a personal relationship with Jesus himself. 2) God does not want to nurse a greedy, selfish baby who doesn't grow for a long time; instead, He desires to have a growing child who maintains person-to-person interaction with Him. The Word of Christ commands the hearer's loyalty to be subject to the sovereign will of God and to His fatherly grace. This is the gift of the Holy Spirit, creating life and obedience. (Brunner, 1952:108) We need to teach the self-negation dimension of faith, as well as the privileges we enjoy as the children of God, and to invite people to dedicate themselves to God.

The divine family is a warm community where people attain new identity and growth in their personal relationship with Jesus. It might be a first priority for the Japanese churches to rediscover the living realities of communion with Christ and fellowship with believers.

9.1.3 Family Enterprise

Swyngedouw (1985) points out that some Japanese companies mobilize the gods for their growth. They employ the dynamism of unity, which the New Religions also tap into, as part of their management practices. The motif of unity in religion is not only found in the New Religions; it is also found in the traditional Japanese community, united like an organism centered on the belief in the productive power of *kami*. Even a majority of those companies that do not relate to the New Religions maintain relationships with some religion to a certain degree. It seems that behind the growing Japanese economy has been a modification of the traditional belief in the production power and dynamism of unity. The religious dynamism of unity is utilized in competition between companies.

Such an intense competition between goal-oriented groups did not develop in Japan until after 1868, when the Meiji government abolished hereditary social ranks and established a capitalist free market. Kato calls this new value orientation "competitive group consciousness." He writes that "Japanese society can be distinguished from that of the West by its strong group orientation; it can be distinguished from that of much of the Third World by its strong competition." (1987:88) This consciousness, that a group should show solidarity toward a common goal and compete together against the outside world at the grass-roots level, has emerged during this modern era. We call this "mission consciousness."

It is interesting to note that companies employ the religious dynamism of unity in order to facilitate their mission consciousness. Japanese supernaturalism, characterized by worship of life-giving power, plays a vital role in the rapid economic growth in Japan.

This mission consciousness may be seen as overlapping with the Pauline view of the community as the "saints" and with Berkof's understanding of the Church, when he says that the apostolic task can only be performed if the Church's being-in-world is a being-different-from-world. Christ's Church is holy because she lives her life in the constant presence of Jesus Christ. However, it should equally be said that her life is lived concurrently within the world. The community of faith neither lives indifferently to the world, nor claims that she has already passed beyond earthly life into the heavenly realm. The community has transferred from the fallen world into the new reality in this world. She is "Christ's dedicated people," living differently within the world.

In order to perform the mediating function, the Church needs to have an agenda for the world, just as Japanese companies plan their own management strategies, yet it should also constantly be aware that this planning itself is the activity of the Holy Spirit. (We will discuss this issue in the next chapter.) Christian churches in Japan have a lot to learn from Japanese secular companies in terms of how to function as a mediator between God and the world.

The church in Japan may be pictured as a family enterprise. She is to be a goal-oriented group, united in one faith in Christ and in love for the family. Each member of the family enterprise is to have a mission consciousness and to work in the world in an integrated way because her president is Jesus, who is a supreme group leader.

9.2   Holy Place

The second image of the Church is as a "holy place," which conveys the institutional aspect of the Church. This image conveys at least two concepts. One is a "window of the spiritual world" and the other is the "point of battle."

9.2.1   Window of the Spiritual World

The Japanese view religious facilities as both centers of religious power and windows of the spiritual world. They are arenas at and through which the spiritual world and the power of the *kami*, Buddhas and other entities may be contacted, encountered, and assimilated for human benefit. It is here that the worshiper moves from the ordinary world into something special, into the powerful presence of the spiritual realm. Spiritual power is usually mediated through statues, prayers, priests and rituals, or by direct supplication.

Visitors are informed that they are entering the realm of the holy and the presence of the *kami*, or Buddhas, by *torii*, a Shinto gateway, or *sanmon* or *niomon*, the Buddhist temple gateways. Many religious facilities have a *temizuya*, a place for ablution, which usually includes a fountain of running water, where visitors rinse out their mouths and wash their hands to cleanse themselves of pollution and evil. At temples there are the ferocious stares of the *nio*, and incense burners at which people may light sticks of incense as offerings, waving the smoke over themselves in a ritual gesture of purification which reinforces the purifying motif. Within the religious arena are numerous objects that illustrate the presence of the spiritual world, such as subtemples, subshrines, and images of animals (as guardians or messengers of *kami*). Shrines and temples are settings at which unusual concentrations of power have shown through and been manifested in the physical world.

Paul describes the church as the temple of God and the indwelling of God. In the church, people are confronted with Christ. She is a place, space, and home where they are welcomed and led to Christ, where they are nourished, shaped and renewed.

For the Japanese, there is a possibility of developing the idea of church as a window of the spiritual world, or a power center, where the One dwells who is overwhelmingly more powerful than *kami*. Christian communicators may be able to appeal to the Christian church as an arena where they may encounter the most powerful God. He fills all things (Eph. 4:10) and they are invited to be filled with all the fullness of God (Eph. 3:19). They can experience the all-embracing and all-transcending power and grace of Christ (Eph. 2:7). The church can represent and exhibit the fullness of Christ, sharing as His body in the place and power of Christ, its Head who fills all in every way (Eph. 1:23).

9.2.2 Point of Battle

As the result of such spiritual interaction in Japanese religious facilities, worshipers receive answers to cope with malevolent spirits. Shrines and temples are recognized as the place where the dangerous, polluting spirits are soothed, transformed or removed. Hence, they may be called a "point of battle."

Because of the Church's holiness in society, she fights spiritual battles. Her battle is not "against human beings but against the wicked spiritual forces in the heavenly world, the rulers, authorities, and cosmic powers of this dark age" (Eph. 6:12). The Church can be seen as a barracks from which soldiers are equipped and sent out. The Church is the God-established, Christ-directed, and Spirit-animated institute of salvation. And

> salvation is not exclusively forgiveness of sins, it also involves deliverance from the dominion of darkness to a realm in which Jesus is recognized as *Kurios* of all the universe—the Kingdom of God's beloved Son (Col. 1:13). (Padilla, 1985:27)

It would be attractive for those Japanese who fear unhappy spirits to regard the Church as the institution of salvation from the dark powers.

The Church needs to be seen as the holy place where spiritual blockages and hindrances are removed by the authority of Jesus' name through the Cross. This is the point of battle where the Kingdom of God invades the kingdom of Satan. In the church, people see the reality of the battle in which Christians are engaged. The Church is the focal point where the glory of God manifests: "the blind can see, the lame can walk, the lepers are made clean, the deaf hear, the dead are raised to life, and the Good News is preached to the poor." (Matthew 11:5)

Christian communicators work as loyal priests not only in the Church but also all over the world as sent from the church. In this sense, the Church is Ezekiel's temple from which a river flows toward everywhere in order to make creatures live, bear fruit and heal (Ezekiel 47:1-12).

Wagner correctly warns against the church's "bless me!" trap:

> While the Church rightly functions as a hospital for healing the wounded, it must also be seen as a barracks for the warriors. It is a place for teaching, training, equipping and spiritual conditioning. It is a place where people are filled with the Holy Spirit and power not simply to bless me but also to be witnesses for Jesus in Jerusalem, Judea, Samaria and to the uttermost parts of the earth. The Church does what healing is necessary but the primary function of the healing is to build up the troops for moving out to the front lines in Kingdom ministries of all kinds. (Wagner, 1992:115)

9.3 Conclusion

We redefine the Church by proposing two images: "divine family" and "holy place." The former communicates three concepts/images, which are "empowered people," "living communion," and "family enterprise." The latter includes two concepts/images, which are "window of the spiritual world," and "point of battle." These notions are designed to provide answers for Japanese questions in conversation with Pauline ecclesiology, consulting contemporary ecclesiology.

In the next section, we examine the concrete figure of the contextual church in Japan based on this ethno-ecclesiology.

Part IV

A Contextual Church
Model for Japan

Chapter 10

Communication Strategies

Our next question, after developing the images/concepts for a Japanese church, is "how can we embody these images/concepts in a concrete setting?" In order to answer this question, we deal with two important issues in this chapter. First, the relationship between the work of the Holy Spirit and human planning, and next, the theoretical framework for developing communication strategies for winning the Japanese to Christ.

10.1 Holy Spirit and Strategies

Some Christians may assume that a Christian partnership with God does not require human planning. They are apt to conclude that the best they can do is to pray, fast and seek the higher spiritual gifts. Is this idea biblically sound?

In this section, we treat the relationship between the aspect of the Holy Spirit and strategic plans in terms of Christian communication.

10.1.1 The Work of the Holy Spirit

Christian communication is a spiritual work. The constant power source of our communication is the Holy Spirit. The communication link is prayer. As Søgaard points out, this involvement by the Spirit is not a "cooperative effort" between God and human beings, as if there were areas of our lives outside of His control:

> It is not a question of God and me each making a contribution, but rather, it is a question of the indwelling Christ working through his body, the church, and its individual members. It is an incarnational concept, Christ in us, working through us (Col. 1:27). It should be an obvious foundational, constant factor permeating all our understanding. (Søgaard, 1991:19)

The Spirit controls the whole process of Gospel communication. The Holy Spirit enables Christian communicators to know, speak, interpret and judge or appraise spiritual truths.

Both Christian communicators and receptors must be placed into dynamic interaction with the Holy Spirit. Only through the dynamic operation of the Holy Spirit will the hearts of both communicators and receptors be opened to the Word of God. The power of the Holy Spirit with the Word of Christ reaches deep into the unconscious, even into the organic and physical realm. God's impact on human life penetrates these depths of the soul, touches these hidden energies, and mobilizes and harnesses them in the service of his Holy Will.

> The Holy Ghost seizes the heart, not merely the *nous*: it pierces the heart until it reaches the depths of the unconscious and even the very physical constituents of personality. (Brunner, 1952:48)

It is not the Christian communicator but the Holy Spirit himself who attracts people to approach to God. Søgaard presents a good illustration in citing Bishop Anderson's words, that the lives of the Christian communicator should be like the sailing boat, dependent on the wind of the Holy Spirit to give it power and speed. (Søgaard, 1991:19) The Spirit uses the Christian community to invite people into a personal relationship with God. The supernatural power of the Holy Spirit, who transforms people's lives, attracts people irresistibly to the Christian community. When people would like to share in this new dimension of life and power, they enter the zone in which the Spirit operates. The spiritual work is comparable to the attractive force of a magnet or the spread of an infectious disease. (Brunner, 1952:52)

People tend to seek double-sided manifestations of spiritual power: the Holy Spirit maintains the quality of daily life of the believers, as well as liberates them to practice and demonstrate the power of the Kingdom. Kraft (1989:168) writes, "What the fullness of the Holy Spirit brings is power (Acts 1:8)—the power to be like Jesus and to minister like him," and mentions the two-sided but simultaneously integrated nature of the Holy Spirit's work.

From the viewpoint of "body ministry," it can be said that the Holy Spirit makes the fellowship, consisting of many separate individuals, into a unity, a single "body," and equips each individual member to perform their own particular work of service. The Holy Spirit lays a firm foundation of lay evangelism for the Christian community, because He encourages people to recognize the mission task as the responsibility of *all* believers, and lets them practice their testimony in their place of work and in their daily life.

Thus the task of the communicator is in tune with the will of the Holy Spirit. Earnest prayers are indispensable factors in Christian communication because it is a spiritual battle. Wagner (1990:46) asserts, "The more deeply I dig beneath the surface of church growth principles, the more thoroughly convinced I become that the real battle is a spiritual battle and that our principal weapon is prayer." Christian communicators must be in tune with what God is doing and how God wants it done. They are instruments in God's hand for the task of communication. They can fight and overcome the power of darkness that hinders communication solely by receiving wisdom, power and endurance from God. Therefore, planning a prayer ministry should be treated more seriously by the local church.

In the next section, we will deal with the planning of strategies. However, it is noteworthy that any goal setting in Christian ministry is "a statement of faith." (Dayton and Fraser, 1990:14) A strategy causes us to seek the mind and will of God when we depend on the work of the Holy Spirit. The church as a family enterprise will develop Spirit-led strategies to touch Japanese heartstrings.

10.1.2 Planning Strategies

The Holy Spirit uses communicators and speaks through them in a supra-logical way, and at the same time in a logically recognizable way. He can work through the mental capacities he has given them to develop plans and carry out communicational activities. Barth explains the dialectical reality of the Church: "That human planning and speech and faith and love and decision and action are also involved according to the divine will and order is also true. This is not compromised by the reference to the secret of the growth." (Barth 1958 in Van Engen 1991:135) Goal-setting, members' activities, leadership, and administration enable the communion of saints to build themselves in missionary work in the world.

In fact, the term "strategy" has deep roots in Scripture. God is working within a strategic framework. He called a specific nation, Israel, at specific times for specific purposes. Jesus selected a small and specific group of people, Galileans, training them and sending them out with a specific commission. The Holy Spirit selected a specific person, Paul, to go to the Gentiles. In the book of Proverbs, God-given principles and wisdom are found. (Engel and Norton, 1975:39)

The Church today also needs a strategy, a way of reaching an objective, a kind of map of the territory to be covered. The Holy Spirit uses well-planned human preparation in doing the work of the Kingdom of God. In many contexts, the absence of planning inhibits the work of the Spirit. The most important matter is the balance between human thinking and God's actions. Developing a strategy involves not only the study of Scriptures, prayer and reliance on the work of the Holy Spirit, but also data collection, research and analysis. In the whole process of the ministry, strategy is required.

10.1.3   Strategy Planning Model

God's way of communicating the message of His Kingdom is similar to the activity of farming. Illustrations of the farmer in the Bible help us to understand how to prepare, sow, cultivate, reap and multiply the harvest for God. Dayton and Fraser provide a circular strategy development model making it relate with the steps of the farmer's work. (Figure 19 on the facing page)

A detailed explanation of the model is not being given here, but the following point is crucial: steps Christian communicators take are to be Spirit-guided. "Because God has called us to a ministry and mission, we need to engage ourselves in the process of discovering his wisdom. Then we must devise a strategy in tune with that wisdom." (Dayton and Fraser, 1990:37)

Research seems to be one of the most neglected areas in all of the missional processes in Japan. Christian communicators need to understand just who it is they are aiming to reach with the gospel. Sincere engagement, studying the receptors, and in particular their economy, worldview, politics, working situation, and religion, will affect their response. Secular companies in Japan spend a great amount of money on field research. The following words of Jesus suggest how the Church should its financial resources for Christ:

178

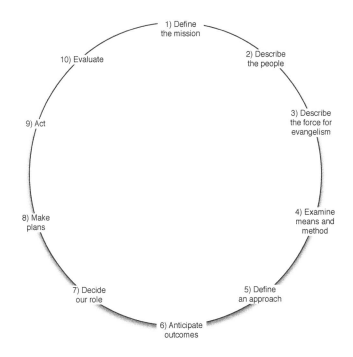

Figure 19: The Planning Model (Dayton and Fraser, 1990:32)

> The master commended the dishonest manager because he had acted shrewdly. For the people of this world are more shrewd in dealing with their own kind than are the people of the light. I tell you, use worldly wealth to gain friends for yourselves, so that when it is gone, you will be welcomed into eternal dwellings (Luke 16:8–9).

Our confidence is that careful thinking bathed in sincere prayer and dependence upon the leading of the Spirit will enable a Christian communicator to reach the target audience.

The Church can be described as a Spirit-filled divine family and as a holy place, which is the temple of the Spirit. She cannot go beyond the Spirit, who is her life. However, it does not mean that she does not have to plan strategies. She needs God-given strategies and their careful development under the guidance of the Holy Spirit.

10.2 Theoretical Framework of Communication

Before discussing the church's concrete strategies for reaching Japanese in the next chapter, we briefly look at four theoretical frameworks to develop the strategies: 1) receptor-oriented communication, 2) felt need, 3) set thinking, 4) person message.

10.2.1 Receptor-Oriented Communication

God's communication is receptor-oriented and it is hoped that Christian communication would be also. Charles H. Kraft defines this concept as follows:

> We recognize the loving nature of God in his communicational activity. To love is to seek the best for the recipient at whatever expense to the source. To love communicationally is to put oneself to whatever inconvenience necessary to assure that the receptors understand. We call this "receptor-oriented communication." This is God's approach and should be ours. (Kraft, 1991a:15)

God is seeking to reach His receptors by entering into their frame of reference. God loves each person and invites them to have intimate fellowship with Him. In order to communicate His loving will to people, He participates in their frame of reference; that is to say, God bends down to disclose Himself through people's ordinary situations. He reaches across the gap between his abode to where the people are. Scripture testifies that an infinite, sinless omnipotent God traverses the communication gap between Himself and finite, sinful, weak human beings through His incarnation. God Himself "became a human being" (John 1:14, Phil. 2:7) to cross that gap once and for all.

We tend to misunderstand the human role in the redemptive work of God. God seeks from human beings a response to Himself. However, He does not require them to construct the bridge; that would be impossible. Human beings can only accept the fact of salvation which God has provided. Kraft explains it impressively:

> The perspective of this book understands God not as one who speaks or reveals "out into thin air," but as one who comes all the way

> to human beings where they are. In crossing the gap between himself and his creatures, God does not merely build a bridge halfway across, calling to us to construct a structure from our end to span the unspanned area. Rather, God employs our language, our culture, the principles of communication in terms of which we operate. He reveals himself in a receptor-oriented fashion. (Kraft, 1979:169)

The Incarnation represents God's personal participation in the lives of his people. God, who exists totally free from culture, chooses to submit to cultural limitations in order to become completely relevant to the human context. God could require human beings to climb up to His sphere and receive his eternal message, but He does not, and instead gives Himself to human beings in personal interaction. Human beings (receptors), who are totally immersed in culture, depend on their limited perception to understand God's revelation. Therefore, God attempts to present Himself by a personal interaction within the receptor's frame of reference. He chooses to work through the cultural vehicles that are at the receptor's disposal.

Jesus is the perfect example of this communication. He had the right to remain God, but became human to dwell among us.

> He thus became a real human being among us—a learner, a sharer, a participant in the affairs of humans—no longer simply God above us. Nor did he then merely content himself to do God-type

things near us. He spent approximately thirty-three years truly among us—learning, sharing, participating, suffering; seen, heard, touched; living as a human being among human beings and perceived by those around him as a human being. He learned, as the book of Hebrews contends, how to sympathize with human beings by allowing himself to be subjected to the temptations and sufferings of human beings. (See Hebrews 2:10, 17-18; 4:15; 5:8, and elsewhere.) (Kraft, 1979:174)

Unfortunately, we sometimes notice that a Christian communicator does not employ the receptor-oriented communication principle. I recently read an article in a secular American newspaper whose author is a representative of a mission organization; he said that to be a Christian means to be a human being. Although the content of the article was logical and interesting to me, I wondered if it provoked contempt from the non-Christian readers. Some of them must have received the message that non-Christians are not human beings. This article was written for the purpose of evangelization, but its effect was to disturb the process of communication. What the readers received was more important than what the writer intended to communicate. Christian communicators should follow God's way of communication.

10.2.2   Felt Needs

Kraft explains the concept of felt needs by saying:

Apparently few if any human beings are completely and permanently satisfied with what

183

and who they are. And no cultural system or life-style appears to provide answers for all of life's questions. Those problems perceived to be uncared for or inadequately dealt with by one's cultural system result in what are commonly referred to as "felt needs." Such needs may be felt at the surface level or at deeper levels. Surface level needs, such as the needs for food, shelter, money, transportation, and the like, are usually easy for a person to articulate.

Deep-level needs, such as the need for someone to care or for some ultimate cause to be involved in, though they may be felt very keenly, are, however, often beyond a person's ability to articulate or even to recognize. wise communicators seek to discover those needs that respondents feel, particularly at the surface level, and to adapt their message so that they perceive the message as relevant to their felt needs. (Kraft, 1991a:68–69)

Luzbetak (1988:162) asserts that "societies will accept only so much of the Gospel as they feel they need." Christian communicators can reach the point of contact for further communication only when they meet the receptor's felt need. A communicator needs to scratch where the receptor perceives that there is an itch before he/she will ordinarily be allowed to dig for deeper itches, because the communicator must gain permission to enter the respondent's private space by dealing with what the respondent permits him/her to deal with. (Kraft, 1991a:69)

Jesus provided many excellent examples of communicating to deal with the receptor's felt need before leading him/her to deeper perceptions of need. He did not say to those who felt a need of healing, "Your real need is not physical but spiritual, so you have to treat your sin first, and after doing that you will have a right to ask to be healed." Sometimes Christian communicators tend to be biased against the receptors' needs without sufficient insight and refuse to listen to them. Or, even if they grasp their needs, the communicators simply ignore them, asserting that their real needs are actually deep spiritual ones. However, in those cases, they not only miss the point of contact but also lose their credibility, something which is indispensable for effective communication.

In many cases, it was the warm acceptance of Jesus that allowed people to open their hearts to him. For example, Jesus never pointed out greed and cheating to Zacchaeus, but accepted him as he was. Jesus never discussed with Zacchaeus the concept of the salvation for a son of Abraham, but simply became a guest of a sinner. Jesus dealt with the receiver's reality, no matter what the objective reality might have been.

John chapter four presents a beautiful story. When Jesus saw the Samaritan woman walking towards the well where he was resting on his journey to Galilee, the Father showed him what her felt needs were. She did not want to have to keep coming to the well to draw water. She had to go there during the hot midday, since she was an object of social contempt due to her failed marriages. So she chose that time to avoid other women. Jesus talked about the living water which would become a spring of water welling up to eternal life in those who drink it. Jesus was so wise that he treated her felt need first and then led her to the deeper truth. The Christian communicator's strategy should be like that of Jesus.

Kraft (1991a:69) explains the normal process of a communicator's involvement in a receptor's felt need.

1. the identification of a felt need and the agreement by both interactants that it is indeed a felt need,

2. dealing with the felt need, and in the process,

3. identifying and raising to the level of felt needs one or more deeper needs,

4. dealing with one or more of these, and

5. discovering and then dealing with one or more others as the process continues.

For people who have power-oriented felt needs like Japanese, rationalistic approaches simply don't work. How many Japanese have responded to the Campus Crusade's "Four Spiritual Laws"? A relatively low number. Christian communicators have to learn how the New Religions have attracted so many young Japanese. The newly developed religion called the Science of Happiness started with four people five years ago, but now has grown to become a two million member group. Ogata points out that several new religions, including the Science of Happiness, are part of the New Age Movement and these have been meeting the supernatural-oriented needs of many people. He also criticizes Christianity in Japan.

> Most of Christianity in Japan is of the old Westernized Christianity with emphasis on its theology and doctrine. It is rational, logical and morally oriented. And it has often excluded the supernatural areas such as healings, miracles, etc. It is this spiritual dimension which the New Age Movement stresses. (Ogata, 1992:6)

How can Christian communicators in Japan meet the felt needs of the Japanese people?

10.2.3 Set Thinking

Hiebert has discussed human thought patterns with regard to categories called "bounded sets" and "centered sets."

Bounded Sets and Centered Sets

A bounded set is a mental category made up of things that share a common set of characteristics. If we define a Christian in terms of bounded set categories, we list characteristics such as acquiring certain knowledge, subscribing to a certain creed, keeping required rites, or observing essential behavioral practices. A Christian's central task then is to maintain the boundary, and the important thing in becoming a Christian is seem to be entering the category. The problem with this understanding is that it will always distinguish Christians from non-Christians on the basis of the presence or absense of certain definitive characteristics, allowing little or no focus on the very important process of growth. Bounded sets do not focus on the process part of decision making and growth.

On the other hand, a centered set approach enables us to form mental categories and words in another way. They are defined by their relationship to a center or frame of reference outside of themselves. A Christian is defined on this model as one who is moving toward Jesus Christ. The crucial thing is not a set of behavioral characteristics or beliefs but a person's growth in allegiance and response throughout the whole of one's life to Jesus Christ as Lord. The central issue is who our God is, and how we relate to him.

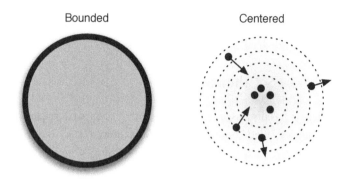

Figure 20: Bounded and Centered Sets (Hiebert, 1978:27)

> Centered sets are dynamic sets. Two types of
> movements are essential parts of their struc-
> ture. First, it is possible to change direction–to
> turn from moving away to moving towards
> the center, from being outside to being inside
> the set. Second, because all objects are seen in
> constant motion, they are moving, fast or slowly,
> towards or away from the center. Something is
> always happening to an object. It is never static.
> (Hiebert, 1978:28)

Centered sets allow us to evaluate the direction of
the movement one takes. Christian advocates should focus
on turning the direction of the Japanese toward the center—Christ. This is the first task that needs to be done for
the unreached people. The unnecessary requirements imposed
by bounded set thinking before one is considered to be a
Christian serve to alienate people from the Christian faith.

The Danger of Fuzzy Centered Sets

Although centered sets express well the relational dimension of Christianity and are a useful approach for Christian communication, there is a danger. The centered sets may become fuzzy centered sets.

Fuzzy sets are characterized by having indistinguishable boundaries. Since the exact area they cover does not begin along a rigid, well-defined edge, they can be understood more in terms of a process having an inexact beginning and end. Because fuzzy sets defy precise categorization, they can easily overlap other sets and blur traditional distinctions. Thus, a conversion to Christianity based on fuzzy set thinking may be an incomplete event. The possibility looms that a convert may embrace, for example, the tenets of Buddha and Christ coterminally.

If a Christian were defined in fuzzy-set terms, there would be no sharp boundary between Christian and non-Christian. People could belong to two or more religions at the same time. They might participate in both Buddhism and Christian services, for example, or combine Shinto and Christianity in responding to the needs of life. Those consequences might be common problems in polytheistic cultures. Hiebert writes,

> Conversion to Christianity in fuzzy-set terms might not be a decisive event. It could also be a gradual movement from outside to in, based on a series of small decisions. (Hiebert, 1983b:426)

A fuzzy-set approach raises even more serious theological and missiological problems. How does one deal with religions

189

such as Hinduism based on fuzzy sets that deny our claims of the uniqueness of Christianity? The Bible makes a clear distinction between the children of God and the children of darkness (Joshua 24:15; Luke 16:13; Col. 1:21–22; and 1 John), and between those who have and have not turned to Christ as the Saviour. If we contextualize the Gospel into fuzzy-set terms, have we not lost an essential part of the Gospel? (Hiebert, 1983b:427)

Set Thinking in Japan's Context

Hiebert's arguments, while being crucial to the mission field in Japan, must be evaluated in light of the following points:

1. Centered set thinking enables us to see God's will, in terms of His desire to draw people into a personal interrelationship with Him. Japanese Christianity is very moralistic. This has been influenced by American puritanism and grown historically out of the context of Bushido (the way of the warrior). It tends to put an unnecessarily high boundary before the people to conserve its ethical traditions such as no drinking, no smoking, and offering a tithe. These requirements for the initiation into Christian life communicate to the Japanese that Christians are unapproachable people who live in a different world. Likewise, Christians also tend to shun Japanese cultural customs. A paradigm shift is needed for Biblical Christian communication which communicates a God who invites sinners as they are.

2. In a pantheistic, supernatural-oriented context like Japan, there usually is a danger of fuzzy sets. People

appreciate any power sources which meet their this-worldly oriented needs. Christian communicators need to challenge these people who live by the logic of their context at a certain point in their decision process to pledge allegiance to the unique Christian God.

3. However, it is not practical that a communicator reflect the negative effects of the fuzzy sets strictly by his/her strategies. Japanese have to be taught the Biblical concept of the only sovereign God over a long period of time. For the initial steps of the learning process, their understanding might be that Jesus is a more powerful god than all other *kami*. This is acceptable until they reach a deeper comprehension of the characteristics and existence of the Christian God. As Van Lueeuwen (1972:145) writes,

> The uniqueness of Christianity can only be experienced by one who believes that in the authentic human personality of Jesus of Nazareth God becomes redemptively, universally and hopefully, present in history, thus definitively inaugurating God's reign for all men and all history.

In Japan, where the Christian influence has not been very strong, one should not expect in many cases to see an instant decisive reaction toward the message.

Fuzzy centered sets are not ideal; however, they may work until the Japanese reach a certain degree of receptivity. Because of God's faithfulness, Christian advocates should cautiously avoid the use of fuzzy sets, but because of God's patience, they should also be ready to accept the whatever initial steps they see from their Japanese receptors.

Therefore, the initial step a receptor will take, in the cognitive dimension, can be described as "awareness of one more powerful than *kami*." If this step is neglected, the next step, which can be described as "awareness of the uniqueness of God," may not be realized.

10.3   Person Message

In the last part of this chapter, we treat the fact that the communicators are the most significant component of the messages they convey, consulting Kraft (1991a:38–51), because there is no greater strategy than the life involvement of the communicator. The receptor pays attention not only to what the communicator says but also to how he/she lives. Communication is not to be equated simply with accumulating information. Personal participation in the lives of the receptors is required because the deeper meanings of the message can only be expressed through shared life involvement between communicators and receptors. How can we communicate the message if we do not earn credibility as respectable human beings?

God's message is a person message. He has communicated His message through person-to-person interaction. He meets individuals as persons. He did not simply input knowledge to human beings, but lived a life among His receptors. And finally, He gave Himself to us by becoming a human being in Christ Jesus. Jesus Christ came not as an angel but as a person who shared our flesh and blood and our weaknesses and, therefore, as one who could be understood by weak human beings.

Jesus is God but he, as a person, interacts with other persons. He interacts with each person as one who lives in his/her particular situation and never in terms of abstract philosophy. For he is sensitive to the concerns each person has, and he rejoices with those who rejoice and mourns with those who mourn (Romans 12:14). When Jesus saw Mary and Martha weeping, "he was deeply moved in spirit and troubled" (John 11:33) and wept. This is not a 'communication technique,' but a natural expression of his loving nature. When he lived among the poor, his disciples understood that the Father loved the poor and invited them to himself. His life was a message from God the Father to his disciples.

Jesus takes our questions seriously. He challenges us to do his will and expects our response. He is a skilful planter who sowed a seed of truth in our heart and reaped our allegiance to him. He also opens himself to two-way communication. His approach to the Samaritan woman in John 4 was a perfect communication situation. In his conversation with this woman, he seems to be pleased with her honest reactions and leads her to ask the right questions in the conversation.

The life of Jesus is our model to follow. He did not establish a seminary. He taught his disciples by providing himself as an example. When he died on the cross, his message of "If anyone would come after me, he must deny himself and take up his cross daily and follow me" (Luke 9:23) is realistic and persuasive. His attitude was summarized in the following words:

> I, your Lord and Teacher, have washed your feet,
> you also should wash one another's feet. I have

> set you an example that you should do as I have
> done for you (John 13:14-15).

Jesus said to the people, "You are the light of the world" (Matthew 5:14). We should note that this is also referring to the person. He did not say, "Your message is the light of the world." Paul describes the same meaning using the image of a letter (2 Cor. 3:2-3).

The quality of the daily life of the communicator is crucial in God's communicational strategy.

> Through the testimony of love, of the in-
> ward peace proper to those who are reconciled
> through the Cross, of their unfailing joy in
> the midst of sorrow, through the power which
> knits the brethren into a unity, through their
> ready sympathy with the distresses and needs
> of others, through the willingness to make per-
> sonal sacrifices understood as a self-explanatory
> consequence flowing from the sacrifice of Christ
> (Brunner, 1952:108)

The person message is the primary way to communicate the gospel in Japan. Explanation of logical principles will hardly attract them, and questions about transcendence like "who is the creator?" will be ignored by the majority. In order to create receptivity, communicators first need to attain credibility as in-group persons for relatively long periods of time. The identity of the communicators is so crucial that what they communicate is secondary. Each lay person needs to be trained in terms of spirituality, character building, and relational evangelism, in order to function as an empowered person who cares and blesses others in his/her place of life.

Mentoring systems and small group dynamics can fit into every decision process of witness and training. Intimate involvements in the receptor's lives in one-on-one relationships or in small groups are necessary settings in developing strategies. Almost every important decision will be made there. People grow into closer relationships with Jesus in the living communion.

10.4   Summary

The church is necessarily limited to spiritual activities, but this does not mean that she does not have to plan strategies. Strategies can be seen as "a statement of faith." (Dayton and Fraser, 1990:14) A strategy causes us to seek the mind and will of God when we depend on the work of the Holy Spirit. The Holy Spirit uses good human preparation in doing the work of the kingdom of God. The task of the communicator, then, is to be in tune with the will of the Holy Spirit. The church needs God-given strategies and their careful development under the guidance of the Holy Spirit.

We have treated four issues making up a theoretical framework to help us develop communication strategies:

Receptor-oriented communication   Receptor-oriented communication is God's approach, and should be ours. We are seeking to reach our receptors by entering their frame of reference.

Felt needs Christian communicators can reach the point of contact for further communication only when they meet the receptor's felt need. We need to deal with power-oriented Japanese felt needs.

Set thinking Centered set thinking enables us to see God's will with the desire to draw people into a personal relationship with him. For the initial steps of the learning process, the understanding of the Japanese people might be that Jesus is a more powerful god than all the *kami*. This is acceptable until they reach a deeper comprehension of the characteristics and existence of the Christian God.

Person message Communicators are the major component of the messages they convey because there is no greater strategy than the life involvement of the communicator. Especially in Japan's person-oriented context, mentoring systems and small group dynamics can fit into every decision process of witness and training.

Chapter 11

Encounters on a Decision Process Model

The aim of this chapter is to suggest a model of strategizing in a contextual church in Japan. "Models are not reality, but they help us understand reality. They are not finite or exclusive, but they serve as frames of reference." (Søgaard, 1989:172) We first discuss two spiritual decision process models, the Engel scale and the Søgaard scale; second, we will deal with Kraft's three encounters in Christian witness; and finally, we will examine how these encounters emerge on the spiritual decision model in Japan's case.

11.1 Decision Process Model

God starts with human beings where they are at, and it is extremely important to know where our receptors are at on the decision continuum. Some Christian communicators use only one method of communicating the Gospel—that is, they expect an immediate response or decision to their message. This is especially true during evangelistic crusades. This method may work for some people, but to use this approach only is to limit the communication potential of the Gospel, because decision making by the receptors is a process and should be recognized as such.

11.1.1   Spiritual Decision Process

The following scale has been presented by James F. Engel. It represents an attempt to relate the communication ministry to the spiritual decision process that occurs as one becomes a believer in Jesus Christ and grows in the faith. Engel contends that everyone will fall somewhere on the continuum represented in Figure 21 on the next page, because everyone is at some stage of awareness of the Gospel or spiritual growth. But for most Japanese, the step of awareness of the supreme being would come later. This scale might, therefore, need to be revised for supernaturalistically-oriented people.

Engel and Norton (1975:46) write,

> Each person's spiritual journey is a lifelong deci-
> sion process. It may begin many years prior to the
> point when a decision is made and one becomes
> born again, or regenerated, in the Biblical sense.
> There usually is a complex of influences in this
> process and these must be understood.

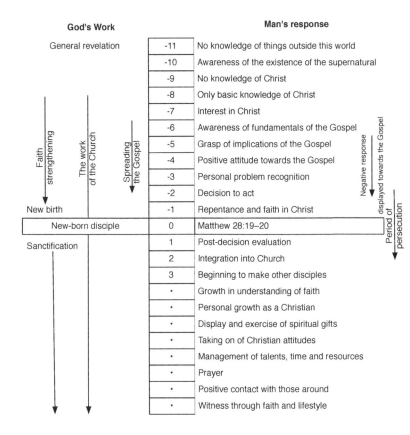

Figure 21: The Spiritual Decision Process (Engel and Norton 1975:45; Faircloth 1991:66)

> The responsibility of the Christian communi-
> cator is to approach people where they are in
> terms of their spiritual position and, through an
> appropriate combination of message and media
> to cause them to progress in their decision pro-
> cess toward initial commitment and subsequent
> growth. The goal, in short, is to bring about
> demonstrable and measurable change in people
> with respect to their response to the gospel.
> (Engel and Norton, 1975:46)

The perspective of the spiritual decision process model
helps the communicator to be aware of what is happening in
the process of the response of the receptor. If a communicator
is to approach some receptors who are passing through different ongoing processes, he/she will have to develop different
strategies and approaches for each one. The communicator can
plot the position of his/her audiences on the model.

The Engel scale, however, is too knowledge-oriented to
apply in Japan's context. He assumes that the communicator's
role starts from the proclamation of the message. This might
work in the Western context, whose historical heritage has
been Christianity, but for the Japanese people who have
no concept of a unique absolute God outside of the world
and whose felt need is extremely power-oriented, Christian
communicators should take a different kind of role when
raising the initial awareness of the Gospel.

11.2   Søgaard Scale

Viggo Søgaard developed the Engel Scale into a two dimen-
sional model for more accurate descriptions. The aim of this

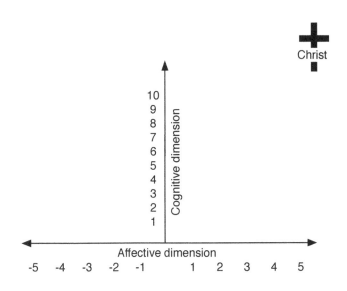

Figure 22: The Søgaard Scale (Søgaard 1991:55; Robb 1989:44)

scale is also to plot the positions of the receptors in their spiritual journey and to plan a ministry to move them toward Christ and on to full maturity in Christ. However, it covers affective changes as well as cognitive changes. The Engel Scale only models a knowledge/persuasion decision sequence. The Søgaard Scale is more wholistic and workable because of its affective dimension, which consists of attitudes and feelings.

Søgaard's two-dimensional model provides a grid on which mapping can take place. The scale consists of two axes, as depicted in Figure 22. The vertical axis is the cognitive dimension, which depicts the people's knowledge of Christ

201

and his gospel. The main difference from the Engel scale is that there is no fixed conversion point, as the decision for Christ can, theoretically, take place at any stage of the cognitive level. Søgaard tries to cover the practical case that people may accept Christ even at a very low level of Biblical knowledge. An affective dimension is added as the horizontal axis, which describes a person's feelings toward the gospel, toward the church and toward Christ. Degrees of negative attitude are pictured on the left and positive on the right.

The journey towards spiritual maturity, our ultimate goal, becomes a journey from one's present position towards the upper right hand corner of the model. In this strategic framework, the communicator analyzes the position of his/her receptors, develops strategy, and plans the necessary ministries to lead people on in their spiritual journey. We will come back to treat a concrete model for reaching Japanese after studying encounters in Christian witness.

11.3   Encounters in Christian Witness

As Tippett (1971:81) points out, "in a power-oriented society, change of faith had to be power-demonstrated." For some people, their spiritual journey begins with information and knowledge, but others will begin their spiritual journey as a result of a power encounter which then leads to attitude change. In fact, large portions of the world's populations are more concerned with questions of spiritual power than with any of the other issues raised in the process of Christian witness. "Among the 88 percent of those classified as unreached peoples, it is estimated that 135 million are tribal animists and

1.9 billion are involved in a world religion based in animism." (Kamps 1986:6, cited in Van Rheenen 1991:25)

The term "power encounter" is used to label healings, deliverances or any other visible, practical demonstration that Jesus Christ is more powerful than the spirits, powers or false gods worshipped or feared by the members of a given people group. (Wagner, 1988:150) Power encounter allows the communicator to make an effective impact on people who have power-oriented needs.

The effectiveness of power encounter in Japan's context is demonstrated by at least one historical precedent and two currently growing movements. Noteworthy is the remarkable healing ministry of Rev. Fujito Tsuge in the Taisho era. (Saijo, 1981) Through his ministry, during a period of only four years (1923-27), over 122,000 came to know the Lord, 60,000 received healing and 22 churches were established. (Saito, 1991:17)

The phenomenally growth of the New Religions give credence to the effectiveness of power encounter. As already stated above, the growth rate of the newly developed religion The Science of Happiness is amazingly high. New Religions meet the supernaturalistically-oriented Japanese felt needs.

Another example is the growth of the Pentecostals and charismatics. Mitsumori (1989) indicates that, among 5,700 Protestant churches, only 7.0 percent are Pentecostals and charismatics. But these churches have increased their membership by almost 34 percent during a recent four-year period (1984–1988). This growth rate is the largest among all Protestant churches. This information implies that a ministry of healing can touch the needs of Japanese.

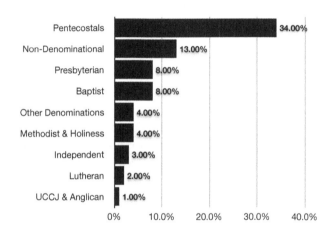

Figure 23: Growth Rate of Churches in Number (1984-1988) (Mitsumori, 1989)

An approach made through miracles may open a way into one of the deepest parts of Japanese worldview, Japanese supernaturalism. The reason is because the impact of the miraculous tends to break "the wall of resistance" (Foster, 1973:18) that the Japanese have and creates an atmosphere of receptivity.

Power demonstrations, however, have at least two goals. Kraft (1991a:5–6) believes that Jesus' power demonstrations were intended to point to something beyond the mere demonstration of God's power:

1. Jesus used God's power to demonstrate God's love.

2. Jesus sought to lead people into the most important of the encounters, the allegiance encounter.

The framework for the essential message is the relationship between God and humankind. God's fundamental desire is to have his people love and obey Him. Jesus talks about the "believer" who did mighty works but was not accepted by God. He said,

> When that Day comes, many will say to me, "Lord, Lord! In your name we spoke God's message, by your name we drove out many demons and performed many miracles!" Then I will say to them, "I never knew you. Away from me, you evildoers!" (Matthew 7:22–23)

The major concern of the Christian communicator should be to prepare the Church as pure virgin who is fully and purely devoted to Christ (2 Corinthians 11:2–3).

The problem of what Kraft calls "dual allegiance" is a practical issue in a supernaturalistically-oriented society like Japan. Kraft writes that "dual allegiance" or "bifurcated Christianity" happens either

A. When people come to Jesus but continue to depend on other spiritual powers for protection, healing and guidance. (e.g. the continuance of dependence on shamans and pagan, Buddhist or Hindu priests, amulets, sacrifices and pagan, Buddhist or Hindu rituals.)

B. When people add to their Christian commitment a dependence on occult powers. (e.g. Freemasonry, New Age, Eastern Martial Arts, fortune telling, astrology, horoscopes, psychic healing) (Kraft, 1992:2–3)

When we start to demonstrate the superior power of Christ through healing and deliverance campaigns, we may attract many people, as the New Religions do. However, those accustomed to accepting power from any available source will not pledge a special and unique allegiance to Christ. For their lasting conversion to Christ, we need to advocate biblically the other two encounters as well: the allegiance encounter and the truth encounter. The purpose of allegiance encounters are to rescue people from wrong allegiance and bring them into relationship to Jesus Christ. Truth encounters are to counter error and to bring people to correct understandings about Jesus Christ. (See Kraft 1991b.)

We need to develop a balanced approach. Those who are attracted to God by the demonstration of God's power (power encounter) may be led to the belief that God is worthy of trust because the Christian God is willing to free people

206

from the destructive power of *kami*. But there need to be other encounters as well: truth encounters and allegiance encounters. The receptor's mind should be challenged through truth encounters to obtain an adequate understanding of the person and purposes of God. Their will should also be challenged through allegiance encounters to bring them into a relationship with God and into a process of growth in intimacy with and likeness to him. Through these encounters they are changed to be like Jesus in person and in ministry, conforming to His image.

In the name of Jesus Christ and by the power of the Holy Spirit, Christian communicators should heal the sick, bless people with peace, seek protection for people from their harsh situations, and rescue people from the control of the disastrous *kami*. All three encounters need to be in balance. All three encounters are intended by God to be integral to every stage of His interactions with humans. (Kraft, 1991b) Only through this total strategy can we avoid the dangers of syncretism and Christian immaturity.

In Japan's context, the main places where these three encounters occur are small group settings and/or one-on-one situations. Because of their worldview themes of contextual logic and groupism, relational evangelism and pastoring are the most functional approaches to take. Establishing credible relationships within small groups is a major premise to evangelize and disciple the Japanese people. In the area of leadership training and mentoring, we should expect to see an informal training model, which can be further defined as a relational experience wherein one person empowers another by the transfer of God-given resources. Clinton points out:

> Already there is momentum for this informal, in-service training model. The Japanese have aspects of mentoring already embedded in the society. But it has not been exploited for Christianity. Instead, formal centralized training was imported from the West. (Clinton, 1991:19)

Kraft describes another dimension of power encounter that should always be integrated with power confrontation, whether in deliverance ministry, healing or other demonstrations of Christ's power:

> Although we do not call them power encounters, our demonstration of love, acceptance, forgiveness, and peace in troubled times—plus a number of other Christian virtues—play the same role of attracting attention and leading people to trust God. These all witness to the presence of a loving God willing to give abundant life and bring release from the enemy. (Kraft, 1991b:262–263)

We include these encounter(s) in the first stage of the witness function of allegiance encounter in our modified Kraft model for Japanese. (Table 8 on the next page.)

Each encounter functions both as a witness to unbelievers and to aid the growth of the believers. The witness function of each encounter can be divided roughly into two categories according to the setting where it takes place: one-on-one settings and in a nurturing small group. Witness in one-on-one settings occurs in the communicators' work place, school, or home, wherever they have contact in their ordinary life

		Starting point	Process	Object
Truth Encounter	Witness function	Display the truth	Think about the truth	Know about the existence of a more powerful God
	Small group witness function	Know about the existence of a more powerful God	Increase of knowledge	Know about the uniqueness of God
	Growth function	Know about the uniqueness of God	Teaching	Understand the truth
Faithfulness Encounter	Witness function	Meet felt needs	Living proof in daily life	Decision to seek God
	Small group witness function	Decision to seek God	Proof of harmony	Trust in Jesus
	Growth function	Trust in Jesus	Growth through relationships	Heights of virtue in Christ
Power Encounter	Witness function	Raise an interest	Proof of power	Response of faith
	Small group witness function	Response of faith	Protecting	Healing
	Growth function	Healing	Greater freedom	Victory over Satan

Table 8: Process of Encounters

besides in church. The seekers who have been witnessed to in one-on-one settings are guided to the decision to participate in a nurturing small group, where they are expected to receive further communication. The growth function in each encounter is also performed in two kinds of small groups: one is for leadership training, the other is for ministry. These divisions are not exclusive. We will discuss them in detail along with the receptor's decision process in the next section.

11.4 Encounters on the Decision Process

We divide the whole decision process into six segments. (See Figure 24 on the facing page.) Point A on Figure 24 indicates the position of the receptor before ministry and point B indicates the decision to visit a church. The first stage is between point A and point B. Point C indicates the decision to come to church regularly. In the same way the second stage is between point B and point C. Point D is the decision to participate in a small group. Point E indicates the decisive allegiance encounter. Point F is the decision to participate in a ministry team.

With Japanese, affective change usually precedes cognitive change. It is difficult for Japanese to receive knowledge-oriented information until they reach point D, which indicates the decision to participate in a nurturing small group. They need to go through the step to be led into the allegiance encounter for the group first before the allegiance encounter for Jesus himself. Wise communicators will then focus on attitude changes in stages one, two and three as the result of power encounters and allegiance encounters. The

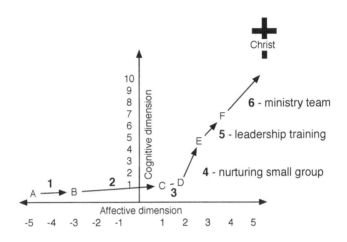

Figure 24: Decision Process Model for Japan

truth encounters should be mainly experienced based on the established personal relationships in the small group and/or mentoring system.

Kraft explains three methods that people use to interact communicationally with others.

> In public communication, the technique employed is usually monologue. With small groups a dialogue or discussion approach is ordinarily most satisfactory. For very small groups or individuals the most effective is what I call life involvement. (Kraft, 1991a:60)

In a local church setting, monologue takes place in a worship service, dialogue in a small group, and life involvement in a mentoring system. How these three approaches help the receptor's spiritual journey in each decision process is examined in Figure 25 on the next page.

Each stage in Figure 24 should be understood as the arena of God's interaction with receptors as well as that of the communicators. The communicators must adapt their methods and programs to meet the changing needs of their receptors.

In stage one, the receptors have not come to church yet. The only practical way to approach them is by mentoring. However, the mission-oriented worship service where communicators are empowered for relational ministry, and intercessory prayers in the small group (which may happen in a ministry team for intercession) help the individual ministries. Life witnesses with power and love in the area of their lives encourage the receptors to decide to visit church. The church functions as an "empowered people" or "children of *kami*" and as a "family enterprise."

In stage two, the receptors are attracted by the indigenized worship and rituals of blessing, which we will cover in the next chapter. They see the gracious, powerful *kami* dwelling in the church and, thus experience the holiness and power of Jesus, who provides life-giving power. In the small group after the worship service they have opportunities to receive blessing, healing ministries, and deliverance ministries. The church functions as a "window of the spiritual world" and a "point of battle." Power evangelism works as the primary attraction and "entry point" to the masses of Japanese due to their supernaturalism. Special healing ministries operate to attract the Japanese people's attention, demonstrate God and lead to the belief that God is worthy of trust. When the

		Worship	Small Group	Mentoring
1	Witness	Worship	Intercession for non-Christian friends	Witnessing by power and love in daily life
	Response	–	–	Decision to come to church

B: Coming to church

		Worship	Small Group	Mentoring
2	Witness	Blessings to raise interest	Demonstration of love	Follow-up
	Response	Receive blessing	Receive love	Decision to come to church regularly

C: Beginning to come to church regularly

		Worship	Small Group	Mentoring
3	Witness	Declaration of grace	Demonstration of love	Counselling, advice
	Response	Hear the message of grace	Receive love	Decision to join a small group

D: Joining a small group

		Worship	Small Group	Mentoring
4	Witness	Declaration of protection, demonstration of harmony	Fundamental teaching	Invitation to trust
	Response	Receive protection	Knowledge of uniqueness of God	Trust in Jesus

E: Regular faithfulness encounters

		Worship	Small Group	Mentoring
5	Witness	Declaration of Christ's victory	Leadership training	Reconfirmation of decision and experience
	Response	Increase in freedom	Decision to join ministry team	Firm trust

F: Joining the ministry team

6	At stage 6, the respondent continues inner healing and growth, and returns to stage 1 the witnesser

Figure 25: Three Approaches in Decision Process

receptors first visit the church, a mentor for each receptor is designated immediately and he/she continues to follow up on them. Loving care by the mentor facilitates the receptors' natural transition to the decision to attend church regularly. It is too early in this stage for the communicators to lead the receptors to limit their activities tho those exclusively related to Christianity. The Japanese are so harmony-oriented that they might try to preserve a harmony with other spiritual power sources and with various groups to which they belong. We have to avoid "dual allegiance." The communicators *must* challenge them to commit to Jesus; however, it is wise to do so only after the receptors receptivity is raised, or otherwise they will quit their spiritual journey at this point.

The focus in stage three is the demonstration of love and warm fellowship. In the worship service, Christ's love is proclaimed. Due to the good fortune consciousness, the Japanese have an ability to discern grace in the ordinary places of their lives. The purpose of proclamation is double-sided: One is to point out the source of the grace; that is, Christ who fills the universe with his all-embracing power. What people can receive is grace and blessing from Jesus, which is greater than the good fortune offered by the *kami*. The other is to point out that grace is manifested in the Church, which is the holy place. The Church is "Christ's fullness." Sincere counseling, care, and intercession within the small group and mentoring demonstrate that the church is the "living communion" where the receptors find their sense of belonging and new identity. Stages one, two and three are preparatory to the receptors' decision to commit themselves to a nurturing small group. This decision is extremely important for them, because it is the place where they are prepared to make a decisive conversion to follow Jesus, not only a more powerful *kami.* The communicators need to establish this stage of commitment to the group before the receptors can commit to Jesus. Having faith in Jesus without the community of faith gives little foundation to support the faith. The Japanese are so group-oriented that they need a community of faith first that attracts them as a warm fellowship (the order for Westerners is the opposite). Receiving faithful care and seeing the life of committed Christians in the small group will serve to promote the receptor's movement toward the next decision point.

The way that receptors grow in their personal relationships with Jesus is by experiencing more of Jesus. This can be augmented through systematic teachings of the essence of the Gospel, provided within the nurturing small group in stage four. Here is where they come to know the unique Christian God and learn to put themselves under his lordship. In other words, they recognize Jesus as the One who deserves to accept their self-surrender. The aim of this stage is to pave the way to face the decisive allegiance encounter where regeneration takes place. Here they learn submission to Jesus, who died for them. It seems to be easy for them to confess their new faith in the one-on-one setting, because of their sense of self-uncertainty, and therefore their mentors need at this stage to invite them to make a commitment to Jesus. Claiming protection is crucial because of the receptors' former relationships to *kami* and/or spirits. The enemy will continue to attack the receptors in attempts to capture, harass and cripple them. Knowing this, the communicators should continue to break the power of the captor that deludes, harasses and causes illness and demonization. By demonstrating harmony in the worship service, Christians can enhance the credibility of the Christian community. (In a later section we discuss how the new rituals express the unity of the community.)

The receptors who are led into this new relationship with Jesus are encouraged to participate in the leadership training program right after their conversion in stage five. They should be trained in a person-oriented post-baptismal care and an apprenticeship-type leadership training program. Leadership training is performed mainly in small groups, but mentoring plays an important role, which is to reaffirm their decisions and experiences. Cooperation between the small group leader for the training and the mentor helps the receptors to integrate their experiences and to attain clear commitment to Jesus. Before completing the leadership training program they are expected to decide to participate in the ministry team. Claiming victory in Christ enables them to receive increasing freedom in physical, emotional, and spiritual realms. The aim of stage five is to equip the receptors for Christian witness.

The receptors are expected to grow towards spiritual maturity. In stage six, the receptors receive on-the-job training in a small group for ministry, such as an intercession team, outreach team, worship team, pastoral care team, or an administration team. Apprenticeship-type training is accomplished in the interpersonal relationships between the leader of the group and the receptors. They are no longer merely the receptors, but become communicators themselves and take some responsibility to minister to those still part of the spiritual decision process.

11.5 Conclusion

In order to develop a workable strategy to communicate the Christian message to the Japanese people, it would be useful to combine the spiritual decision process and encounters-thinking with some communication theory. All three encounters are integral to every stage of the receptor's spiritual decision process. They are intended by God for his interaction with humankind.

A power encounter can begin the spiritual journey toward Jesus for many Japanese, because the Japanese have power-oriented felt needs. This, however, needs to be emphasized in balance with other encounters: the truth encounter and the allegiance encounter. A key for unlocking the Japanese for Christ is to communicate the Gospel with spiritual power, but also with a sense of balance in culturally relevant communication strategies. These encounters can take place in small groups and mentoring systems as well as in the worship service.

The purpose of these strategies is to show the Japanese that Jesus is above all *kami*, and the one who deserves their self-surrender. Fulfilling their felt needs, in terms of both power and community, unlocks the Japanese hidden desire of self-surrender and redirects it to the transcendent God. If the Church in Japan were to re-establish itself along the lines of this new ethno-ecclesiology, it would better serve to move the Japanese along in their spiritual decision processes, to the point where they live and minister like Christ.

Chapter 12

New Christian Rituals

In the previous chapter, mentioned the possibility of creating new Christian rituals to bless, claim protection and demonstrate harmony. The contextualized Christian rituals are discussed here along with a methodology and concrete examples.

As examined in section 3.5 on page 66, one of the Japanese worldview themes is "form consciousness." It must be understood, in a worship service, Japanese people are not familiar with the idea of giving a spontaneous, varied expression of the life that is within them. They need rituals that they can follow and formed patterns of worship that almost all of the worshippers perform together. Contextual ritual is a necessary step for the contextualization of the gospel.

12.1 Critical Contextualization

Hiebert's article "Critical Contextualization" (1984) explains the procedure for dealing with cultural forms in Christian communication.

12.1.1 Denial of the Old

When people become Christians, how should they respond to their past cultural forms: traditional rituals, songs, myths, proverbs or other cultural systems? To reject the old customs as pagan is one common response, and is indeed the path Japanese Christians have so far taken. Songs, dances, customs of ancestor veneration, marriage customs and funeral rites have been condemned because they were thought to be directly or indirectly related to traditional religions or to be immoral.

As a result of the uncritical rejection of Japanese cultural forms and uncritical acceptance of Western cultural forms, most Japanese consider Christianity as a foreign religion. Most Japanese, therefore, must have an image that Jesus is an Westerner who cannot relate to people who live in the unique Japanese cultural situation.

> The importation of cultural practices from outside has made Christianity a foreign religion in many lands, and alienated Christians from their own peoples and cultures. It is this foreignness and not the offense of the Gospel that has often kept people from following Christ. We must be careful not to confuse the two. (Hiebert, 1984:288)

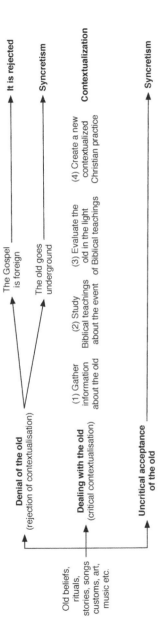

Figure 26: Types of Contextualization (Hiebert, 1984:290)

12.1.2   Accept the Old

A second response to traditional practices is to accept them uncritically into the church. The advocators of this position generally have a deep respect for other cultures; however, they tend to overlook the fact that there are corporate and cultural sins as well as personal ones. An uncritical acceptance of the cultural forms opens the door to syncretism just as the uncritical rejection of them sometimes does.

12.1.3   Dealing With the Old

A third approach to past customs is to deal with them consciously in a process. Hiebert calls this "Critical Contextualization."

> In this the old is neither rejected or accepted uncritically. It is explicitly examined with regard to its meanings and functions in the society, and then evaluated in the light of biblical norms. (Hiebert, 1984:290)

The procedure of critical contextualization is as follows:

1. Become aware of the need to deal with some area of church life.

2. Gather and analyze the various practices that make up the custom under examination.

3. Study the Bible related to the question at hand.

4. Evaluate critically people's own past customs in the light of their new biblical understanding and reach a decision regarding their use.

5. Create new symbols and rites that convey new Christian meanings, in forms understood within their own culture.

12.1.4   Forms and Meanings

How we view the cultural forms is an essential question for contextualization. As shown in chapter 8, the enemy uses cultural forms, and as Hiebert (1989:118) points out, contextualization is not a once-and-for-all task. So that we must cautiously reshape the symbols of culture. If there are corporate sins in conjunction with the forms, the Japanese Christian needs to repent of them. If there is demonic influence, they need to renounce it. However, we believe that most cultural forms are by nature neutral, as Kraft (1979) emphasizes. We take the God-above-but-through culture position, that God intends to use Japanese cultural forms to communicate His loving personality and His lordship in general. Every cultural form was created for God's glory. Therefore, contextualization is the attempt to restore the original purpose of the redemptive gifts of the culture.

Table 9 on the next page is a chart of the relationship of cultural forms and meanings to indigeneity/syncretism.

Indigenous forms combined with indigenous meanings result simply in a traditional religion. A blend or mixture of Christianity with pre-Christian religious beliefs and practices is labeled "syncretism." There are at least two roads that lead to syncretism. One is called "Christo-pagan syncretism," which

223

Forms	Meanings	Result
Indigenous	Indigenous	Traditional Religion
Foreign	Indigenous	Christo-Pagan Syncretism
Foreign	Foreign	Domination Syncretism
Indigenous	Christian	Indigenous Church

Table 9: Relationship of Forms and Meanings to Indigenity/Syncretism (Kraft, 1987a:447)

occurs when people adopt surface level forms from Christianity, while attaching to these forms deep level meanings from their pre-Christian religious allegiances. The other approach is called "Domination syncretism," which happens as a result of domination by outsiders. This occurs when people adopt new practices that have little correlation with their indigenous life and, therefore, have to create new meanings for them. Our aim is to have an indigenous church using indigenous forms to which are attached Christian meanings. The meanings should come neither totally from the sending nor the receiving societies, but from an integrating of scriptural truth and experience into the receptor's lives and cultural practice. Then people will think of the Lord as their own God who meets their needs.

In spite of our sinfulness and limitedness, God intends to communicate himself through the Japanese culture to the Japanese people. On this theoretical foundation, we try to establish contextualized ritual. We need not only a "butter-smelling church," but also a "soy-sauce-flavor church" for the majority of the Japanese people.

12.2 Some Examples of Contextualized Forms

Some examples of contextualized forms are suggested in this section. We believe that some concrete images should be projected in the reader's mind even though this may be only a first small step in a major shift. We propose rituals using water (*mizu*), demarcations of the people and the place with salt (*shio*), and a ritual with hand clapping (*teuchi*), and bowing. (*hairei*)

12.2.1 Water (*mizu*)

Japan is a rainy country, so the imagery of water permeates the various areas of Japanese people's life. We pick up three important functions of water in Japanese culture in order to consider its contextualization.

Blessing from the Source of Life

The first function is the healing and rejuvenating function.

> Every village seems to have its spring or its well, and they all have healing and rejuvenating powers. One such is the *wakasai* (roughly, "well of youth") at Nara, where in the coldest days of winter the priests of Todai-ji gather to draw water in the ritual called *omizutori*. This water is also believed to offer health and youth. In the old days, from this and other wells, the first water drawn on New Year's morning was *wakamizu* or "water of youth." (Liman, 1983:15)

225

The Holy Spirit is associated with water, which gives life cleansing. The New Testament uses water for Spirit in such connections as the following: Fluid-oriented terminology of the Spirit can be found in Luke-Acts ("pour out": Acts 2:17–18, 10:45; "filled": Luke 1:15, 1:67; Acts 2:4, 4:8; Eph. 5:18). John uses water to express his theology of the Spirit (1:32–33; 3:5–8; 7:38–39). The early church believed in and practiced the outpouring of the Holy Spirit (Acts 2:4, 16–21). Jesus announces that he is the source of such "living water" (John 7:38-39). "Water of life" (Rev. 21:6; 22:1, 17) denotes genuine, everlasting life.

Water can become a part of the new Christian rituals for healing. Rubbing oil in the name of the Lord when praying for the sick (James 5:14) can substitute for the pouring out of water. Sprinkling sacred water can be used for rituals of blessing. It may make the receptors imagine the Holy Spirit, who fills them, and/or Jesus who is the source of life. The drawback to using water in a ritual, however, is that an observer might easily assume that it is the water itself that has the power, rather than being merely the vehicle for administering the blessing. It must be pointed out conclusively that water, in and of itself, has no "magic." These rituals are designed according to the structure of the *ketsuke* ritual and scheduled according to the annual cycle and life cycle for intensification. (See Chapter 5.)

Purification

The second function is purification. Shinto worshippers accomplish purification by symbolically rinsing the mouth and pouring clear water over the finger tips, which is called *temizu* (literally, "hand water"). Formal purification is conducted by

226

a priest without using water, (*harai*) yet this ritual is often accompanied by lightly sprinkling salt or salt water. (See Ono 1962.) Purification by bathing is usually called *misogi*. Adherents make their ablutions in the river when they feel they have sins or impurity. This also happens before participating in a major festival.

In the Scripture, water is also used for ceremonial cleansing. Water was assumed to be the primary cleansing agent and to have the power to make one ceremonially clean. The Old Testament ritual for cleaning involves bathing, washing one's clothing and waiting until evening (Lev. 15:5–27; 16:26–28; 17:15; 22:6; Deut. 23:10–11). References to water in the New Testament occur frequently in connection with both Christian baptism (Acts 8:36–39; Heb. 10:22; 1 Pet. 3:20) and John's baptism of repentance (Matt. 3:11; Mark 1:8; Acts 1:5, 11:16). Baptism can be interpreted as an initiatory cleansing ritual, a symbol of inner cleansing (Heb. 10:22).

There is a possibility of using the action form of *temizu* before attending worship, and of *misogi* as an expression of repentance. Baptism by immersion may have special meaning in Japan.

Forgiveness

The last function of water we want to point out is forgiveness. There is an expression to forgive and forget, *mizu ni nagasu*, which literally means "to flow with the water."

A motif of forgiveness was included in the act of foot washing in John 13. Jesus washed the feet of the disciples, even those of Judas Iscariot. It can be viewed as the expression of love and forgiveness to him. Therefore the foot washing service is meaningful in Japan. The ritual participants may be reminded of Jesus' forgiveness for them and decide to forgive others.

12.2.2   Salt (*shio*)

Because salt is important to human life, it has universally acquired sacred, ritual significance, and so it has been viewed in Japan as a means of purification and a source of magical power. For example, it is the general custom all over Japan to have a family member scatter salt at the entrance of the house before the mourners enter, to protect them from contamination through contact with the dead at a funeral. "It has even become a custom in recent years for the family of the deceased to distribute small packets of salt to the mourners themselves for this purpose." (Jenke, 1983:42) The purifying function of salt can be seen in its magical use such as *morijio*, the placing of a small mound of salt at a restaurant entrance to ensure that no evil enters.

Salt was used in the Old Testament in sealing a covenant (Lev. 2:13). The usage of salt in 2 Kings 2:20–21 implies its function as denoting separation from the past and current shift of purpose. Some sacrificial use of salt can be found in Jesus' saying. "For everyone will be salted with fire. Salt is good; but if it loses its saltness, how can you make it salty again? Have salt in yourselves, and be at peace with one another." (Mark 9:49–50). "The salt of the earth" refers to the use of salt as a preservative, keeping things wholesome and worthwhile (Matt. 5:13; Mark 9:50; cf. Col. 4:6).

Christian communicators can use salt to express Christian dedication and sanctification. For example, at the installation service of the church leaders, including lay leaders, or at the baptismal reception, a pastor can sprinkle salt blessed in the Name of Jesus to express their dedication, separation from the world and perseverance of their spiritual quality. We can employ the custom of *morijio* to establish the border of a holy place. People will assume that they enter the holy place when they step over the *morijio*. It should be emphasized again, as in the case of anointing with water and oils, that the salt is symbolic only, and contains nothing of a magical nature.

12.2.3 Hand Clapping (*teuchi*) and bowing (*hairei*)

Ono (1962:59) explains the procedure of Shinto worship in the home. After performing the purification rite,

> the worshipper stands or seats himself on a mat facing the miniature shrine and makes first a slight bow and then two deep bows. Following this whatever comes to mind as a prayer is repeated either audibly or in silence. Two deep bows, two claps with the hands in a raised position at about the level of the chest, a deep bow, a slight bow and the rite is over.

The bow expresses deep respect to the *kami*. This is also true in a secular situation where the bow (*ojigi*) is the most natural expression of a simple greeting, thanksgiving, respect and condolence to another. On the other hand, clapping hands expresses harmony between the worshipper and *kami*. This action was also secularized in the clapping of hands in patterned rhythm, which is called *sanbon-jime*, performed on several occasions that bring about harmony in the group, like seasonal festivals.

In the Bible, the bow is a position of submission adopted toward a superior person or deity for purposes either of petition or worship (Gen. 18:2, 27:29, 33:3; Phil. 2:10). Clapping hands is a sign of acclamation of a king (2 Kgs. 11:12) or God (e.g. Ps. 47:1, 98:8; Isa. 55:12).

We believe that Christian workers can adopt the bow (*ojigi*) for Christian worship to God and the clapping of hands in patterned rhythm (*sanbon-jime*) as an acclamation of Jesus in a harmonious way.

12.3   Summary

Because of the "form consciousness" of the Japanese people, new Christian rituals can have a significance in worship and other religious activities in a contextual church. We mainly employ Hiebert's "critical contextualization" as a methodology for creating new contextualized Christian practices. In creating new symbols and rites, we critically evaluate Japanese religious customs in light of their new biblical understanding. In spite of our sinfulness and limitations, God intends to communicate himself through the Japanese culture to the Japanese people.

Some examples of contextualized ritual are suggested. Water can be used for rites of blessing, purification and forgiveness. Blessed salt can be employed for demarcations of the people and the place. Hand clapping and bowing can be adopted in worship as an acclamation of Jesus.

Part V

Conclusion

Chapter 13

Summary and Conclusions

We conclude this dissertation by 1) summarizing the whole thesis, 2) drawing our conclusions, 3) giving direction for further study, 4) suggesting a possible approach, and 5) presenting an epilogue.

13.1   Summary of the Whole Thesis

An ethno-ecclesiology and a contextual church are required by the nature of God's interaction with the Japanese people. God is pleased with uniquely Japanese expressions of Christian life as they emerge from their own indigenous socio-cultural context, rather than as a transported foreign expression. Only when they have found their own expression of Christian life does the church become vibrant and alive, which leads to what Allen (1962b) called "spontaneous expansion." God intends to communicate His love and will in a receptor-oriented fashion by using Japanese cultural gifts in a contextual church. When this happens, the Japanese will think of the Lord as their own God, who meets their needs and answers their questions. Moreover, God will bless the universal Church through the unique contribution of a Japanese way of living the Gospel and of understanding the Church. God appreciates the diversity of cultures and would like to use the Japanese perspective as other means to reveal Himself to the world.

The methodology of developing a contextual church model is characterized by the establishment of some images/concepts of the church; these images and concepts are products of an ethno-ecclesiology. The ethno-ecclesiology is designed to answer Japanese questions emerging from the Japanese worldview in the light of a Pauline perspective of the Church, consulting contemporary ecclesiology.

Japanese supernaturalism and groupism prompt the Japanese people to ask certain questions. Firstly, "Who gives us life-giving power?" Second, "Who protects us?" And third, "To whom or to what do I belong?" The fourth question is hidden under the surface of pragmatism, which is "How can I reach eternity?" An effective ethno-ecclesiology needs to answer these Japanese questions.

We define the church by giving two images, which are "divine family" and "holy place." The former is the community aspect of the Church and communicates three concepts/images, which are "empowered people," "living communion," and "family enterprise." The Church is the "empowered people" who have access to God's supernatural power and can apply His resurrection power out of love for people who live in fear of spirits. Additionally, the Church is a "living communion" where people attain a new identity and growth in their personal relationship with Jesus. The Church may also be portrayed as a "family enterprise;" she is to be goal-oriented, mission-oriented and united in one faith in Christ and the love of family.

The second image of the Church is as a "holy place," which represents the institutional aspect of the church. It conveys at least two concepts: "window of the spiritual world" and "point of battle." The Church is a "window of the spiritual world" through which the Japanese may encounter the one who is overwhelmingly more powerful than the *kami*, experiencing the all-embracing power and grace of Christ. The Church also needs to be seen as the "point of battle" wherein the Kingdom of God invades the kingdom of Satan. There, spiritual blockages or hindrances are removed by the authority of Jesus' name through the Cross.

In order to incorporate these images/concepts into the Japanese settings, the church needs God-given strategies, and these strategies require careful development. We combine Søgaard's spiritual decision process model and Kraft's 'three encounters' thinking with some communication theory. A power encounter can begin the spiritual journey toward Jesus for many Japanese, because the Japanese have power-oriented felt needs. The power encounter to be emphasized in balance with other encounters: the truth encounter and the allegiance encounter. A key for unlocking the Japanese for Christ is to communicate the Gospel with spiritual power, but also with a sense of balance in culturally relevant communication strategies. Small group dynamics and a mentoring system must be utilized in every decision process.

Due to the "form consciousness" of the Japanese people, creating new Christian rituals has to be promoted as one

235

of the highest priorities for a contextual church. Employing Hiebert's concept of "critical contextualization," we have critically evaluated Japanese religious customs in light of the Biblical teachings, in order to create new Christian rituals. Some examples of the new rituals we suggest are using water, using salt, hand clapping and bowing.

13.2 Conclusions

1. The Church in Japan needs to answer Japanese questions emerging from the Japanese worldview in receptor-oriented fashion, in the light of Biblical teaching.

2. The felt needs of the supernaturalistically-oriented Japanese are to be dealt with in a contextual Church. The Church can be presented as made up of "empowered people" who have access to God's supernatural power. It provides a "window of the spiritual world" through which the Japanese can encounter Jesus who fills the universe. It functions, further, as a "point of battle" where spiritual blockages and hindrances are removed by Jesus' name.

3. Group-oriented felt needs are to be treated in a contextual church. The Church can be pictured as a "living communion" where people attain a new identity, and as a "family enterprise" which maintains a shared unity and mission.

4. The Church must communicate the Gospel with power encounters integrated with truth encounters and allegiance encounters, using small group strategies, a mentoring system, and contextual rituals.

5. The purpose of these strategies is to show the Japanese that Jesus is above all *kami* and, therefore, deserves their allegiance and self-surrender.

13.3 Further Study

We are beginning to ask different questions about the church. Previously we asked either "What does the Bible say about the church?" or "How do German theologians view the church?" or "How can the church raise its voice against the violation of human rights?" All of questions must be asked. Unfortunately, however, these questions have not been effectively integrated, and thus they have failed to bear fruit in missiological terms. The task of constructing an ethno-ecclesiology and a contextual church has just begun.

We need to engage in a wholistic study of the Biblical images and concepts of Church. We have only covered Pauline ecclesiology. We also need thorough studies of contextual church models in other worldwide churches. Japanese worldview and culture must be examined thoroughly in terms of Christian anthropology. In particular, the issues of ancestor veneration must be addressed. Japanese people's felt needs differ according to the generation, social context, and race. There are some oppressed minority groups: Korean, Chinese, aborigines, people from Okinawa and those who are relegated to a strict caste system. In addition, the population of temporary laborers from the Middle East and Asia is rapidly increasing. Planning strategies that pay attention to the various felt needs of these contexts must also be investigated in a receptor-oriented fashion. These must include contextualized leadership training programs. The development of a contextualized ritual church form is currently merely in the beginning stages.

Needless to say, this agenda has to be practiced in the real world. A missiologist is not an armchair theorist, but stands on the ground of actual ministry in the existing church. Our attempt is neither a desk plan nor an academic game. It is the search for a way the Japanese can love Jesus through their own particular Japanese expression. God's joy, manifested from the contextual church out to the world, will be the real proof of the Church's life.

13.4   A Possible Approach

The emphasis of a contextual church should be to present Christ's power and personhood. Christ is not a *kami*, nor is he even the greatest *kami*, but above all of the *kami*—who, in Biblical terms, can be likened to mere angelic powers. But Christ is the Head of all things (Eph. 1:22), of all principalities and powers (Col. 2:10). A contextual church can proclaim and demonstrate Christ's superiority above all rule, authority, power and dominion, namely the numerous *kami* in Japan.

Although *kami* have a certain degree of personality, they are categorized principally as mana, impersonal powers. Christ is not like a *kami* whose main benefit to worshippers derives from the provision of good fortune. Christ is not only a source of cosmos-supporting power—a manifestation of energy—but he is a person who provides God's grace. In other words, Jesus loves the Japanese in a *personal* way. Although fully a person, Christ is not hampered by the imperfect emotions that drive humans toward erratic behavior.

He always seeks the best for us. He actually gave his life for us. Our response to Christ's grace is to trust in him.

How different that is from the Japanese attitude toward *kami*! The Japanese people have to exert a lot of effort in order to maintain a balanced and productive relationship with *kami*. Therefore a contextual church is in a position to suggest a better alternative to attaining life-affirming power: the direct, personal interaction between God and humans characterized by love through grace.

Another crucial aspect involves the accessibility of the Church facilities themselves. Shinto shrines and Buddhist temples are open all day long. People are able to tap into the life energy of *kami* or Buddha whenever they want, while Christian churches in Japan are usually open only Sunday morning and Wednesday evening. This is not a good example of receptor-oriented communication! The Church needs to have a strategy developed out of the receptor's felt needs. A church door that is closed all day unconsciously communicates an insult to the Japanese. A key step that the contextual Church can take, then, is to scratch that surface itch of the Japanese by borrowing wisely from their religious traditions.

In the process of planting the first church in my home town, we are seeking concrete ways of contextualizing Japanese cultural forms into new Christian customs on the basis of a blueprint suggested in this thesis. To do this we plan to recruit church planters and intercessors to help establish a contextual church. We believe that a database and a contextual manual for church planters will be produced as the fruit of the first church planting. These experiences, as well as development of a body of people who are growing with a vision of a contextual church, are expected to be the foundation of widely multiplying, dynamic-equivalence churches. Through development of a contextual church and an effective church planting movement, we might well see a great awakening of the Holy Spirit take shape in Japan.

13.5   Epilogue

Seeking indigenous church forms for the Christian church in Japan is a pioneering work. It may often be criticized by others. First, the pioneers risk the danger of being labeled advocates of syncretism by local church leaders who take a "God-against-culture position," as well as by some missionaries who hold a "God-endorsing-my-culture perspective." Second, the pioneers may be condemned by Evangelical Christians who don't accept the 'power evangelism concept,' regarding it as a new type of Pentecostalism or as some kind of Christianity-generated New Religion. Third, they may be ridiculed by pessimists who don't believe in God's redemptive gifts for the Japanese culture. Fourth, the world church is not necessarily open to highly contextualized expressions of Christianity.

In spite of these potential criticisms by some Christians, we can be positive in our Christian communication in Japan, because such a contextualized church would convey God's message to people living in a uniquely Japanese context. Our conviction is that through working with the Holy Spirit, we can discover God's redemptive gift within Japanese culture and employ it for a better church ministry.

Bibliography

Titles given in square brackets are the author's translation of Japanese titles.

Akata, M. (1986). 祖霊信仰と他界感 *[Briefs in Ancestral Spirits and the Concept of Other World]*, Kyoto: Jinbun Shoin.

Allen, R. (1962a). *Missionary Methods—St. Paul's or Ours?*, Michigan: Eerdmans.

Allen, R. (1962b). *The Spontaneous Expansion of the Church and the Causes which Hinder It*, London: World Dominion Press.

Anderson, R. S. (1992). *The Praxis of Pentecost: Revisioning the Church's Life and Mission*, Pasadena, CA: Fuller Theological Seminary.

Araki, H. (1973). 日本人の行動様式 *[The Behavioral Patterns of Japanese]*, Tokyo: Kodansha.

Arnold, C. E. (1992). *Powers of Darkness: Principalities and Powers in Paul's Letters*, Downers Grove, IL: InterVarsity Press.

Asahi Newspapers (1990). *Asahi Keywords 1991*, Tokyo: Asahi Shinbun-sha.

Baken, P. (1971). The Eyes Have It, *Psychology Today* (4): 64–67.

Banks, R. J. (1988). *Paul's Idea of Community: The Early House Churches in the Historical Setting*, reprint edn, Grand Rapids, MI: William B. Eerdmans.

Barclay, W. (1958). *The Mind of St. Paul*, San Francisco, CA: Harper San Francisco.

Barth, K. (1956). *Church Dogmatics: 4/1*, Edinburgh: T. and T. Clark.

Barth, K. (1958). *Church Dogmatics: 4/2*, Edinburgh: T. and T. Clark.

Barth, K. (1961). *Church Dogmatics: 4/3/1*, Edinburgh: T. and T. Clark.

Barth, K. (1962). *Church Dogmatics: 4/3/2*, Edinburgh: T. and T. Clark.

Ben Dasan, I. (1970). 日本人とユダヤ人 *[The Japanese and the Jews]*, Tokyo: Yamamoto.

Benedict, R. (1934). *Patterns of Culture*, Boston, MA: Houghton-Mifflin.

Bensley, R. E. (1982). *Towards A Paradigm Shift in World View Theory: The Contribution of A Modified Piagetian Model*, PhD thesis, Pasadena, CA, Fuller Theological Seminary.

Berkhof, H. (1986). *Christian Faith*, Grand Rapids, MI: William B. Eerdmans.

Boff, L. (1986). *Ecclesiogenesis: The Base Communities Reinvent the Church*, Maryknoll, NY: Orbis Books.

Bonhoeffer, D. (1963). *The Communion of Saints: A Dogmatic Inquiry into the Sociology of the Church*, New York: Harper and Row.

Bonhoeffer, D. (1971). *Letters and Papers from Prison*, London: SCM Press.

Bosch, D. (1991). *Transforming mission: Paradigm shifts in theology of mission*, Maryknoll, NY: Orbis books.

Brunner, E. (1949). *Christianity and Civilization*, New York: Charles Scribner & Son.

Brunner, E. (1952). *The Misunderstanding of the Church*, London: Lutterworth.

Brunner, E. (1964). *Truth as Encounter*, London: SCM Press.

Clinton, R. J. (1991). Future Perfect Thinking: Will Japanese Leadership Be Ready?, *Global Church Growth* **28**(3): 17–19.

Cohen, R. A. (1969). Conceptual Styles, Culture Conflict, and Non-verbal Tests of Intelligence, *American Anthropologist* 71(8): 28–55.

Conn, H. M. (1984). *Eternal Word and Changing Word*, Grand Rapids, MI: Zondervan.

Cook, F. H. (1975). Introduction of Buddhism to Japan and Its Development during the Nara Period, *in* C. S. Prebish (ed.), *Buddhism: A Modern Perspective*, University Park, PA: Pennsylvania State University Press.

Dale, K. J. (1977). Transforming barriers into bridges, *Japan Christian Quarterly* (53): 153–160.

Dawson, J. (1989). *Taking Our Cities For God: How to Break Spiritual Strongholds*, Lake Mary, FL: Creation House.

Dayton, E. R. and Fraser, D. A. (1990). *Planning Strategies for World Evangelization*, Grand Rapids, MI: William B. Eerdmans.

Doi, T. (1973). *The Anatomy of Dependence*, Tokyo: Kodansha International.

Doi, T. (1990). 信仰とあまえ *[Faith and amae]*, Tokyo: Shunjusha.

Earhart, H. B. (1984). *Religions of Japan: Many Traditions Within One Sacred Way*, New York, NY: Harper and Row.

Engel, J. F. and Norton, H. W. (1975). *What's Gone Wrong with the Harvest?*, Grand Rapids, MI: Zondervan.

Faircloth, S. D. (1991). *Church Planting for Reproduction*, Grand Rapids, MI: Baker.

Foster, G. M. (1973). *Traditional Societies and Technological Change*, 2nd edn, New York, NY: Harper and Row.

Fujii, M. (1985). 仏事の基礎知識 *[Fundamental Knowledge of Buddhist Services]*, Tokyo: Kodansha.

Gilliland, D. S. (1983). *Pauline Theology & Mission Practice*, Grand Rapids, MI: Baker.

Gilliland, D. S. (1989). Contextual theology as incarnational mission, *in* D. S. Gilliland (ed.), *The Word Among Us*, Dallas, TX: Word Books.

Gorai, S. (1986). 古代宗教における海と山 [Mountain and Ocean in Ancient Religion], 神と人―古代信仰の源流 *[Kami and Human Beings: The Roots of Ancient Faith]*, number 58, Osaka: Asahi Culture Books.

Gorai, S. (1991). 日本人の地獄と極楽 *[Japanese View of Hell and Paradise]*, Tokyo: Jinbun Shoin.

Grant, I. L. (1985). Worldview and worldview change: A reader. Class Supplementary Articles MB725.

Hamaguchi, E. (1982). 日本的集団主義 *[Japanese Collectivism]*, Tokyo: Yohikaku.

Hanayama, S. (1991). 葬式法事入門 *[Manual of Funeral Rite and Ancestor Veneration]*, Tokyo: Gomashobo.

Hanson, P. D. (1986). *The People Called: The Growth of Community in the Bible*, San Francisco, CA: Harper and Row.

Hayashi, C. and Yonezawa, H. (1982). 日本人の深層意識 *[The Depths of Japanese Consciousness]*, Tokyo: Nippon Hoso Shuppan Kyokai.

Hayashi, M. (1988). *Learning from the Japanese New Religions*, PhD thesis, Pasadena, CA, Fuller Theological Seminary.

Hiebert, P. G. (1978). Conversion, culture and cognitive categories, *Gospel in Context* 1(4): 24–29.

Hiebert, P. G. (1982). The flaw of the excluded middle, *Missiology: An International Review* 10(1): 35–47.

Hiebert, P. G. (1983a). *Cultural Anthropology*, 2nd edn, Grand Rapids, MI: Baker.

Hiebert, P. G. (1983b). The Category "Christian" in the Mission Task, *International Review of Mission* 72(287): 421–427.

Hiebert, P. G. (1984). Critical contextualization, *Missiology: An International Review* 12(3): 287–296.

Hiebert, P. G. (1985). *Anthropological Insights for Missionaries*, Grand Rapids, MI: Baker.

Hiebert, P. G. (1989). Form and Meaning in the Contextualization of the Gospel, *in* D. S. Gilliland (ed.), *The Word Among Us*, Dallas, TX: Word Books.

Hiebert, P. G. (1990). Phenomenology and institutions of folk religions. Class syllabus MR520.

Hirano, J. (1982). 日本の神々 *[Gods in Japan]*, Tokyo: Kodansha.

Hoekendijk, J. (1966). *The church inside out*, London: Westminster Press.

Honecker, M. (1963). *Kirche als Gestalt und Ereignis [Church as Form and Essence]*, Munich: Chr. Kaiser Verlag.

Hori, I. (1968). *Folk Religion in Japan: Continuity and Change*, Chicago, IL: University of Chicago Press.

Hoshino, K. and Symbol Creation (1991). 全予測１９９２年消費文化はこうなる *[The Overall Prediction of Consumers' Culture in 1992]*, Tokyo: PHP.

Inagaki, H. (1990a). Post Modern Japanism, *Japan Harvest* **1990**(3): 8–14.

Inagaki, H. (1990b). 大嘗祭とキリスト者 *[The Royal Succession Ritual and Christianity]*, Tokyo: Inochi no Kotobasha.

Ishida, I. (1983). 神と日本の文化 *[Kami and Japanese Culture]*, Tokyo: Perikansha.

Ishihara, K. (1976). キリスト教と日本, Tokyo: Nihon Kirisutokyoudan Shuppan Kyoku.

Iwai, H. (1986). 神と人との交換 [The Friendly Exchange between *Kami* and Human beings], 神と人―古代信仰の源流 *[Kami and Human Beings: The Roots of Ancient Faith]*, number 58, Osaka: Asahi Culture Books.

Jacobs, C. (1992). Healing of nations, Lecture at Fuller Theological Seminary on March 25, 1992.

Japan Ministry of Culture (1972). *Japanese Religion*, Tokyo: Kodansha.

Jenke, G. (1983). *Shio* (salt), *Discover Japan Vol. 2: Words, Customs and Concepts*, New York, NY: Kodansha International.

Kajimura, N. (1988). *The Faith of the Japanese*, Tokyo: Chuuou Kouron-sha.

Kamps, T. J. (1986). *The biblical forms and elements of power encounter*, Master's thesis, Columbia Graduate School of Bible and Missions.

Kato, S. (1987). The Sources of Contemporary Japanese Culture, *in* Public Relations Department, Corporate Secretariat Division, Nippon Steel Corporation (ed.), *Essays on Japan from Japan:* 日本の心―文化、伝統と現代 *[The*

Heart of Japan: Culture, Traditions, and the Modern Age, Tokyo: Maruzen Kabushiki Gaisha.

Katsube, M. (1987). The Three Types of Bushido, *in* Public Relations Department, Corporate Secretariat Division, Nippon Steel Corporation (ed.), *Essays on Japan from Japan:* 日本の心ー文化、伝統と現代 *[The Heart of Japan: Culture, Traditions, and the Modern Age*, Tokyo: Maruzen Kabushiki Gaisha.

Kearney, M. (1984). *World View*, Novato: Chandler and Sharp.

Kitagawa, J. (1987). *On Understanding Japanese Religion*, Princeton, NJ: Princeton University Press.

Kraft, C. H. (1979). *Christianity in Culture: A Study in Dynamic Biblical Theologizing in Cross-Cultural Perspective*, Maryknoll, NY: Orbis Books.

Kraft, C. H. (1987a). Anthropology text. Unpublished manuscript, Fuller Theological Seminary, School of World Mission.

Kraft, C. H. (1987b). Worldview and spiritual power. Unpublished manuscript, Fuller Theological Seminary, School of World Mission.

Kraft, C. H. (1989). *Christianity with Power: Your Worldview and Your Experience of the Supernatural*, Ann Arbor, MI: Servant.

Kraft, C. H. (1991a). *Communication Theory for Christian Witness*, Maryknoll, NY: Orbis Books.

Kraft, C. H. (1991b). What kind of encounters do we need in christian witness?, *Evangelical Missions Quarterly* (27): 258–265.

Kraft, C. H. (1992). The Problem of Dual Allegiance: Can People Follow Both Jesus and the Shaman? Unpublished manuscript, Fuller Theological Seminary, School of World Mission.

Liman, A. V. (1983). *Mizu* (water), *Discover Japan Vol. 2: Words, Customs and Concepts*, New York, NY: Kodansha International.

Lingenfelter, S. G. and Mayers, M. K. (1986). *Ministering Cross-Culturally: An Incarnational Model for Personal Relationships*, Grand Rapids, MI: Baker Books.

Luzbetak, L. J. (1988). *The Church and Cultures*, Maryknoll, NY: Orbis Books.

Mainichi Newspaper (1986). 心の時代 [the era of the heart], Mainichi Newspaper, January 4.

Matsugi, N. (1991). 救いの構造 *[The Structure of Salvation]*, Tokyo: NHK Books.

Mayumi, T. (1984). 神道の世界 *[The Shinto World]*, Osaka: Toki Shobo.

Minami, H. (1983). 日本的自我 *[Japanese Self-Consciousness]*, Tokyo: Iwanami Shoten.

Minami, H. (1987). The Japanese Mind, *in* Public Relations Department, Corporate Secretariat Division, Nippon Steel Corporation (ed.), *Essays on Japan from Japan:* 日本の心一

文化、伝統と現代 *[The Heart of Japan: Culture, Traditions, and the Modern Age*, Tokyo: Maruzen Kabushiki Gaisha.

Miner, P. S. (1959). *Horizons of Christian Community*, St. Louis, MO: Bethany.

Mita, M. (1965). 現代日本の精神構造 *[The Mental Structure of Modern Japanese]*, Tokyo: Kobundo.

Mitsuhashi, T. (1984). 厄払い入門 *[Introduction to Yakubarai]*, Tokyo: Kobunsha.

Mitsumori, H. (1989). Growth rate of churches in number, *Japan Update* 3(1).

Miyake, H. (1974). 日本宗教の構造 *[The Structure of Japanese Religion]*, Tokyo: Keio Tsushin.

Miyata, N. (1983). 神と仏 *[Kami and Buddha]*, number 4 in 民俗学大系 *[A Compedium of Folklore]*, Tokyo: Shogakukan.

Moltmann, J. (1977). *The Church in the Power of the Spirit*, New York: Harper and Row.

Morimoto, T. (1991). *Samurai Mind*, Tokyo: PHP.

Muramatsu, E. (1992). 儒教の毒 *[The Poison of Confucianism]*, Tokyo: PHP.

Murayama, S. (1990). 変貌する神と仏たち *[The Changing Kami and Buddhas]*, Tokyo: Jinbun Shoin.

Naisbitt, J. (1982). *Megatrends: Ten New Directions Transforming Our Lives*, New York, NY: Warner Communications.

Nakamura, H. (1989). 日本人の思惟方法 *[Ways of Thinking of the Japanese]*, Tokyo: Shunjusha.

Neill, S. (1957). *The Unfinished Task*, London: Lutterworth.

Newbigin, L. (1953). *The Household of God*, New York, NY: Friendship.

Niebuhr, H. R. (1951). *Christ and Culture*, New York, NY: Harper and Row.

Nishiyama, S. (1984). 現代日本のカルト宗教 [Cultic Religion in Contemporary Japan], *Tama* (34): 64–69.

Nishiyama, S. (1988a). 現代の宗教運動 [Religious Movements Today], *in* E. Omura and S. Nishiyama (eds), 現代人の宗教 *[Religion for Contemporary People]*, Tokyo: Yuhikaku.

Nishiyama, S. (1988b). 現代宗教の行方 [Directions in Contemporary Religion], *in* E. Omura and S. Nishiyama (eds), 現代人の宗教 *[Religion for Contemporary People]*, Tokyo: Yuhikaku.

Nishiyama, S. (1991). Youth, deprivation, and new religions, *Japan Christian Quarterly* 57(1): 4–11.

Nitobe, I. (1899). *Bushido: the Soul of Japan*, New York, NY: Putnam.

Ogata, M. (1985). *Small Group and Leadership Training for Church Growth in Japan*, PhD thesis, Pasadena, CA, Fuller Theological Seminary.

Ogata, M. (1987). 教会成長と聖霊の力 *[Church Growthand the Power of the Holy Spirit]*, Tokyo: Akatsuki Shobo.

Ogata, M. (1992). Handling the Science of Happiness, *Japan Update* **5**(2): 6.

Ohara, S. (1979). 日本人の精神風土とキリスト教 [The Japanese Spiritual Climate and Christianity], 日本人とキリスト教 *[Japanese and Christianity]*, Tokyo: Joshi Paul Kai.

Ono, S. (1962). *Shinto - The Kami Way*, Rutland: Charles E. Tuttle.

Opler, M. E. (1946). Themes as dynamic forces in culture, *The American Journal of Sociology* (51): 198–206.

Padilla, C. R. (1985).   *Mission Between the Times*, Grand Rapids, MI: William B. Eerdmans.

Picken, S. D. B. (1980). *Shinto: Japan's Spiritual Roots*, Tokyo: Kodansha International.

Prince, D. (1990). *Blessing or Curse: You Can Choose*, Tarry Town, NY: Chosen.

Reader, I. (1991). *Religion in Contemporary Japan*, Honolulu: University of Hawaii Press.

Reid, D. (1991). *New Wine: The Cultural Shaping of Japanese Christianity*, Berkeley, CA: Asian Humanities Press.

Ridderbos, H. (1975).   *Paul: An Outline of His Theology*, Grand Rapids, MI: William B. Eerdmans.

Robb, J. D. (1989). *Focus! The Power of People Group Thinking*, Monrovia, CA: MARC.

Saijo, Y. (1981). *Pentecost Before and After: The Autobiography of Rev. Fujito Tsuge, A Servant of God*, Kobe: Kassuishi Henshushitsu.

Saito, H. (1991). Keys to Unlocking Japan for the Gospel, *Equipping the Saints* **5**(3): 17–19.

Saji, Y. (1990). 謎の列島神話 *[The Enigmatic myths of Japan's Islands]*, Tokyo: Tokuma Shoten.

Sakaiya, T. (1991). 日本とは何か *[What is Japan?]*, Tokyo: Kodansha.

Sakurai, T. (1985). 結集の原点 *[Origin of Regimentation]*, Tokyo: Kobundo.

Schreiter, R. J. (1986). *Constructing Local Theologies*, Maryknoll, NY: Orbis Books.

Segundo, J. (1973). *The Community Called Church*, Maryknoll, NY: Orbis Books.

Shaeffer, F. A. (1976). *How Should We Then Live? (The Rise and Decline of Western Thought and Culture)*, Old Tappan, NJ: Fleming H. Revell.

Shaw, R. D. (1981). Every Person a Shaman, *Missiology: An International Review* **9**(3): 359–366.

Shukyo-shakaigaku-no-kai (ed.) (1985). 生駒の神々―現代都市の民俗宗教 *[Gods in Ikoma: Folk Religion in Modern Urbanity]*, Osaka: Sogensha.

Sobrino, J. (1984). *The True Church and the Poor*, Maryknoll, NY: Orbis Books.

Søgaard, V. B. (1989). Dimensions of approach to contextual communication, *in* D. S. Gilliland (ed.), *The Word Among Us*, Dallas, TX: Word.

Søgaard, V. B. (1991). *Communicating the Gospel: Media in Church and Mission*, prepublication edn, Pasadena, CA: Fuller Theological Seminary.

Song, C.-S. (1986). *Theology from the Womb of Asia*, Maryknoll, NY: Orbis Books.

Sonoda, M. (1977). 残響の彼方 *[Beyond Reverberation]*, number 1 in 講座宗教学 *[Lectures in Religious Studies]*, Tokyo: Tokyo University Press.

Spae, J. (1971). *Japanese Religiosity*, Tokyo: Oriens Institute for Religious Research.

Spiro, M. (1984). Some Reflection on the Family and Religion in East Asia, *in* G. A. D. Vos and T. Sfue (eds), *Religion in the Family in East Asia*, Los Angeles, CA: University of California Press, pp. 35–54.

Swyngedouw, J. (1985). 神々の動員ー宗教と経営の一致 [Mobilization of Gods: Union of Religion and Management], Asahi Newspaper, January 28.

Taber, C. R. (1978). Is There More than One Way to Do Theology?, *Gospel in Context* 1(1): 4–10.

Takeda, K. (1987). Archetypes of Japanese culture, *in* Public Relations Department, Corporate Secretariat Division, Nippon Steel Corporation (ed.), *Essays on Japan from Japan:* 日本の心ー文化、伝統と現代 *[The Heart of Japan: Culture, Traditions, and the Modern Age*, Tokyo: Maruzen Kabushiki Gaisha.

Takemitsu, M. (1991). 呪術が動かした日本史 *[The Japanese History Driven By Magic]*, Tokyo: Nesco.

Tippett, A. R. (1971). *People Movements in Southern Polynesia*, Chicago, IL: Moody.

Tsushima, M., Nishiyama, S., Shimazono, S. and Shiraki, H. (1986). 新宗教における生命主義的救済感 [Life-oriented View of Salvation in New Religions], *in* J. Miyake, S. Nishiyama and M. Komoto (eds), 宗教 *[Religion]*, number 19 in リーディングス日本の社会学 *[Readings in Japanese Sociology]*, Tokyo: Tokyo University Press.

Umehara, T. (1990). The Civilization of the Forest, *New Perspectives Quarterly* 7(3): 22–31.

Van Engen, C. E. (1991). *God's Missionary People: Rethinking the purpose of the Local Church*, Grand Rapids, MI: Baker.

Van Lueeuwen, J. (1972). Uniqueness and Universality of Christ, *Unique and Universal*, Bangalore: Dharmann College.

Van Rheenen, G. (1991). *Communicating Christ in Animistic Contexts*, Grand Rapids, MI: Baker Books.

Wagner, C. P. (1988). *How to Have a Healing Ministry without Making Your Church Sick*, Ventura: Regal.

Wagner, C. P. (1990). *Church Planting for a Greater Harvest*, Ventura: Regal Books.

Wagner, C. P. (1992). *Warfare Prayer: How to Seek God's Power and Protection in the Battle to build His Kingdom*, Ventura: Regal Books.

Warner, T. M. (1991). *Spiritual Warfare*, Wheaton, IL: Crossway.

Watanabe, S. (1978). 日本の仏教 *[Japanese Buddhism]*, Tokyo: Iwanami Shoten.

White, T. B. (1990). *The Believer's Guide to Spiritual Warfare: Wising Up to Satan's Influence in Your World*, Ann Arbor, MI: Servant.

Yamaori, T. (1983). 神と仏 *[Kami and Buddha]*, Tokyo: Kodansha.

Yonemura, S. (1986). 家と祖先礼拝 [Family and Ancestor Veneration], *in* J. Miyake, S. Nishiyama and M. Komoto (eds), 宗教 *[Religion]*, number 19 in リーディングス日本の社会学 *[Readings in Japanese Sociology]*, Tokyo: Tokyo University Press.

Yoshino, H. (1982). 日本人の死生観 *[Japanese View of Life and Death]*, Tokyo: Kodansha.

Yoshino, H. (1983). 陰陽五行と日本の民族 *[Yin-yang Magic and Japanese Folk Customs]*, Kyoto: Jinbun Shoin.

Zahrnt, H. (1966). *Die Sache mit Gott: Die protestantishe Theologie im 20. Jahrhundert [The Event with God: Protestant Theology in the 20th century]*, Munich: R. Piper and Co.

Index of Citations